The Catechism of the Catholic Church: *Familystyle*

We Love

Volume 3

David M. Thomas, Ph.D.
& Mary Joyce Calnan

A DIVISION OF TABOR PUBLISHING
Allen, Texas

NIHIL OBSTAT
Reverend Edward L. Maginnis, S.J.
Censor Deputatus

IMPRIMATUR
Very Rev. Donald F. Dunn
Vicar General for the Diocese
of Colorado Springs

October 5, 1994

The nihil obstat and imprimatur are official declarations that a book or pamphlet is free of doctrinal or moral error. No implication is contained therein that those have granted the nihil obstat and the imprimatur agree with the content, opinion, or statements expressed.

ACKNOWLEDGMENTS

Scripture quotations are taken from or adapted from the Good News Bible text, Today's English Version. Copyright © American Bible Society 1966, 1971, 1976, 1993.

Excerpts from the English translation of the *Catechism of the Catholic Church for the United States of America,* copyright © 1994, United States Catholic Conference, Inc.—Liberia Editrice Vaticana.

DESIGN: Davidson Design

Send all inquiries to:
Thomas More Publishing
200 East Bethany Drive
Allen, Texas 75002–3804

Printed in the United States of America

ISBN 0–88347–297–X

2 3 4 5 6 00 99 98 97 96

Contents

Foreword

It is the tradition of families to hand down their most treasured possessions from one generation to the next. Each new generation accepts the special gift with great reverence, because it connects the family with its history, identity, values, and stories.

It is in this tradition that the family which is the Church has treasured the gift of faith and the inheritance that the Creator bestows on us as the children of God. The gift of faith has been treasured and preserved down through the ages in the stories of Scripture, the teachings of the Church, the writings of saints and scholars, the celebrations of sacramental life, and the witness of lives of love and service.

In this spirit, our Holy Father Pope John Paul II convoked an extraordinary assembly of the Synod of Bishops in 1985 which began the task of drafting a compendium of Catholic doctrine to insure that the inheritance of our faith story, values, and traditions would be accessible to and suited for the generations of the present and the future. The *Catechism of the Catholic Church* is primarily a resource of doctrinal, moral, social, and spiritual teaching for all those who have been given the responsibility of passing on our faith inheritance.

David Thomas and Mary Joyce Calnan have taken the *Catechism* down from the shelf, as it were, have given it life, and have made it an inheritance that will be passed down from family to family, from generation to generation. Their four-volume *Catechism of the Catholic Church: Familystyle* is the first local or national catechism written from the original resource. They are faithful and careful stewards of the Church's treasure of faith and values. First, they have divided their familystyle catechism into the same divisions as the *Catechism of the Catholic Church*—Creed, Sacraments,

Life in Christ, and Prayer. Second, the reader can follow the development of topics in the same order as the new *Catechism*. Third, they connect the doctrine of our faith to the reality of life today in a process and style that touches your heart and your spirit. By adapting the *Catechism* to the culture and lifestyle of the family, they "unwrap" the *Catechism* and allow us to know our God as intimately caring and as connected to our everyday lives.

David and Mary Joyce are exemplary disciples of the Master Teacher as they skillfully and sensitively tell extraordinary stories of ordinary people, which draw you into the Word of God in Scripture and into the particular teaching of our faith tradition. Each chapter invites the reader to reflect on story, Scripture, doctrine and then to apply this to his or her own life as a family member. Each chapter concludes with a prayer for the rich resource of Church tradition adapted to the language and life of the family. Although this resource is intended primarily for families in all the many shapes and forms of family systems today, I believe that the *Catechism of the Catholic Church: Familystyle* will be a special gift to everyone in catechetical, liturgical, and other pastoral ministries as a resource and as a spiritual companion.

I am deeply honored to be invited to write the foreword for this book. David Thomas and Mary Joyce Calnan have a rich background in family life ministry. Their *Catechism of the Catholic Church: Familystyle* reflects that ministry as this work brings faith to life and life to faith. I know that readers will join with me in expressing my deepest gratitude for this gift of faith and love that will undoubtedly become a new classic in American Catholic spirituality.

Howard J. Hubbard
Bishop of Albany, NY

Introduction

You have just opened the third book in a series of four. This volume focuses on our Christian life and on the decision making moments in our lives. Moments when we have both freedom and responsibility—freedom to choose and responsibility to make choices from the very center of our being, the place where God dwells and calls us to love. It builds on Volume One, *We Believe,* and Volume Two, *We Celebrate.*

The four volumes of the *Catechism of the Catholic Church: Familystyle* correspond to the four parts of the *Catechism of the Catholic Church* recently issued by the Vatican. Pope John Paul I requested that the catechism of the whole church be adapted to local churches. This we have done as we here connect the life of the family with part three of the Vatican's catechism, "Life in Christ."

Choices are from the place where God dwells.

This volume is about morality. It's about those times in family life, along with the rest of our life, when we freely act from a place of how Jesus would act. Plain and simple. Big and little decisions. Big and little mistakes. Learning, always learning. Always on a journey and never, ever alone. Our God dwells always within us, there to help us up should we fall down. And always, always, our God is filled with love and understanding.

We too are called to love. In this volume, through family language and experience, we talk about how we are to love as our God loves us. In the words of Jesus, this is the greatest of all the commandments, so great that it contains all the rest.

Let us begin.

CHAPTER ONE
The Call to Happiness and Holiness

They would celebrate every year, hoping . . .

They were used to the ritual: They'd give the little kids their hot dogs early, and everyone else would have chicken from the grill later. They'd put the container for the beverages over by the trees; then they'd put the tablecloths on the two tables and move them together. They'd put up the net for the bigger grandkids and set up the portable crib for Matthew or Alex, in case their parents wanted to put them down for a nap.

"Let's see," she said out loud to the kitchen, "the salad's all set, the beer and wine are in the refrigerator, all I need to do is put the chicken in the marinade—but not 'til later, so now I'll go help Dad."

Everyone was coming! Well, almost everyone. Joan, the oldest granddaughter wouldn't be with them because she was off with her friends. Her mother didn't like the fact that she wasn't coming to the annual gathering at Grandma and Grandpa's. But the older couple understood. Kids grew up and out!

"Hi, Gramma! Where's Grandpa?" the first arrival blurted out. He always dashed from the car and hurtled through the kitchen door long before the rest of the family! He was never at a loss for things to do while he was there. In fact, he orchestrated the other little kids.

"Hi, Ryan, give Gramma a kiss" she greeted him, "Does your mother need help?" But he was gone in a flash, and so she stepped out on the porch just as two more cars pulled up, loaded with the rest of the family.

In no time, they were off and running! Every family member was used to the annual ritual. Each seemed to know her or his role or chore, and just went on automatic to do it. The only thing that really changed every year was the topic of conversation! What they talked about each year depended on the factors in everybody's life and on politics and sports. The rest was just family being family—again.

"Grandpa, are you ready to play ball with us?" one of the kids asked. So the eldest person present grabbed his trusty old mitt and headed to the front yard to keep the middle children out of everyone's way. He was used to this!

But every year he enjoyed his role and his grandchildren; and every year new ones joined and others no longer played. But Grandpa was always there.

"Wow! what a hit!" he exclaimed numerous times. And "Great try!" other times. But always, always the game progressed toward the moment he got up to bat. And then they all had the best time of all! Because Grandpa couldn't hit the ball. (At least in front of these kids he couldn't, otherwise he'd ruin the game!)

Finally, chow time arrived! Time for the annual massive consumption of food!

Every year, when the get-together was over, the family swore that next year they'd move to a local park. But they knew they never would. Getting together wouldn't be the same that way.

And deep down, in everyone's hearts, they knew that the only ending to this would be when Mom and Dad could no longer manage the day and the ballgame and the gathering. And they all knew that day would eventually come. But until then, they would celebrate every year, hoping in their hearts that the next year would come.

In the beginning the Word already existed; the Word was with God, and the Word was God.

The Word was in the world, and though God made the world through him, yet the world did not recognize him. He came to his own country, but his own people did not receive him. Some, however, did receive him and believed in him; so he gave them the right to become God's children. They did not become God's children by natural means, that is, by being born as the children of a natural father; God himself was their Father.

Out of the fullness of his grace he has blessed us all, giving us one blessing after another. God gave the Law through Moses, but grace and truth came through Jesus Christ. *John 1:1, 10-14, 16-17*

In family we learn to be church.

The *Word* in John's Gospel means Jesus, the promised one. His coming fulfills a promise God gave to the Jewish people. The Hebrew Testament records this promise. Again and again in the Bible, God gives God's word that someday a messiah would come to the Hebrew people. But when Jesus did come, many did not believe that he was in fact God's word fulfilled, and so they did not become Christians. Some still waited for God's word to be fulfilled.

We Christians believe that God's word came to fulfillment in Christ Jesus. As Christians living out our faith within the Catholic church, we accept and celebrate the fact that God made the Word flesh and that Jesus—God's word made flesh—dwells among us. We also believe that God has never abandoned us. Jesus died, was raised from death, and eventually ascended to his Father. However, our loving God sent the Holy Spirit to be with us always. Jesus promised this; he told us that he would not leave us orphans.

As people born into this present reality, God invites each of us—one by one—to discover, accept, and live the message of Jesus. Easy to say. Sometimes hard to do.

For most of us, our life as a Christian began when our caregivers—parents or others—brought us into the domestic church through baptism. That was the beginning. The hard work came/comes later. As caregivers ourselves, we must teach and model Jesus' way, truth, and life for our own families. We must take Jesus' words and actions—his life—to heart. Only then will we model our own lives on Jesus' life. Such is the Christian journey, which begins at baptism, continues throughout our life, and reaches perfection after death.

God calls all of us to seek and find the living God. God's promise to us is fulfilled in our discovering—over and over again—the meaning of Jesus' life and death and resurrection. Thus, we go deeper and deeper into the mystery of God's love and become more and more Jesus to those we know and meet. We begin to radiate Jesus to others. We begin to love through thick and thin. Although this can happen in all our relationships, the opportunity to love is most often found in our family relationships. In family we learn to *be* church.

The family in our opening story is being church. Eager to gather together to celebrate and commemorate a longtime family ritual, they honor and ensure the continuity of this way of being family. They pass on to the children the value of creating opportunities for family to be family.

And what is family? Food and laughter and games and more food and dirty diapers and scraped knees and sobs and teasing Grandpas and concerned Grandmas and, often, selfless love. There is happiness and holiness—just as God intended. For this is family at it's very ordinary holy best! Hot dogs and all.

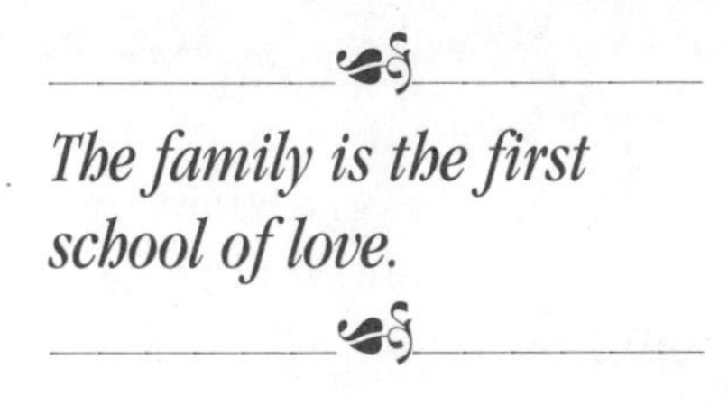

The family is the first school of love.

This small book of the familystyle catechism is about the way we live and the way we love. It's about how we express—through our daily decisions and actions—all we deeply treasure in our lives We enter life with a strong hunger or desire for complete and total happiness. As we journey, we discover that God and those who reveal God to us—family, friends, other loved ones—are the happiness we seek.

Jesus came to be with as and to share with us a message—that God loves us unconditionally and that God is present to us each moment of every day. The Scriptures identify Jesus as the word of this loving God—the word that gives and proclaims life. Through our connection with Jesus, we receive a new identity and a new name—Christian. Signed in Christ's name, we become God's adopted children, members of God's own family. As God's children, we long to live in such a way that our actions will reveal God's loving presence in the world.

As we live the life of Christians, a life modeled on the way Jesus loved and served others, we become like God, that is, we become holy. *Holy* simply means that we become sacred because God's life flows through us and around us and within us. The more we live and act as children of God, the holier we become. And out of this holiness can come great good for the world, just as out of Jesus' holiness came redemption for the world.

With holiness comes happiness and goodness. The three are like facets of one diamond, a diamond that is ourselves. God desires us to be happy and holy and good. God longs for us to be precious gems through which the love and life of God shines.

That's the big picture, the picture of our entire life. But we must break down this big picture into its parts. And what are those parts? The ordinary, everyday events of our life. Out of these come goodness and holiness and happiness. They come from God being with us—now and forever.

Our moral life

Growing up we were told what to do.

When do we begin our acquaintance with morality, our sense of the difference between right and wrong? Probably even earlier than when a two-year-old is told that it's not nice to bite. What's right and what's wrong, perhaps mostly the latter, brings us to memories of growing up when we were told what to do. Parents, teachers, priests, nuns, law enforcement officers, and the school nurse gave us orders: Do what we tell you to do! Obey. If you follow directions, you won't be hurt. You will not go to hell. You will be loved. "She's such a good little girl." "He's such a good little boy, he does everything he's told."

An exaggeration? Perhaps. But others do teach us, give us guidelines about what's right and what's wrong from the very beginning when we are little. It is in our family that we first learn about morality and most everything else we know about being human. If we are to be holy and good and happy, we need to learn to love. And the best way to learn to love is by being loved. That's why the church describes the family as the first school of love.

Jesus said that the world would know his followers by the way they loved. As family members we all know that genuine love is demanding. Jesus died because he loved so deeply. And we look to Jesus as the source for our understanding of right and wrong.

Jesus as the way, the truth, and the life

Jesus did much more than tell us how to live. He showed us how to live, how to love as God loves. His was a life of service that led finally to death and then to resurrection.

Jesus was human, real, alive.

Jesus was human, real, alive. And he came to us as God's word in personal form. We don't know how much time he spent thinking about good and evil, right and wrong. But his words and actions certainly show us where he stood with regard to right and wrong, to love and nonlove.

He believed that humans find deep happiness in doing good. But his description of what's good was often contrary to the culture of his time and ours too! For instance, Jesus said that those who were poor in spirit would be happy.

Now, thinking that happiness—in our world's terms—comes from being poor in anything presents difficulties! However, that's how the section in Matthew's gospel begins as it describes what we call the beatitudes. Some translations of the Bible use the word *beatitude* with the word *blessed*. For example, "Blessed are the poor in spirit . . ." and so forth. We might call the beatitudes the "Be attitudes." What do they mean by that play on words? That when we are *be*ing Christian, we have certain attitudes within us.

When we live in the way described by the beatitudes, we are blessed. That is, we grow closer to God. And happiness comes when we are close to God. The cutting edge of the beatitudes is that they describe a way of being and a way of living that often differ dramatically from the way most of the world lives.

The world says we will be blessed and happy if we are rich—especially if we have large sums of money stored in Swiss bank accounts! For the world, happiness is knowing that we can buy anything we want and doing just that! Rich is "in" and poor is "out." These attitudes are a far cry from the blessedness of the beatitudes.

Life in the kingdom

Kingdom living happens in ordinary life.

Jesus offers a way of living, of relating, and of loving that is radically different from the world's way. His words and his deeds reveal the difference. Jesus announced to us that new possibilities, new challenging options, exist for us because we can be part of the kingdom of God. Life in the kingdom is not business as usual. The demands of this kingdom may be difficult, but the rewards are great—true goodness, happiness, holiness. Love to last a lifetime and beyond. Hunger fulfilled.

The foundation for life in the kingdom is living in love, which means living generously and responsibly. It also means letting go of those aspects of life that are incompatible with life in the kingdom. What does this mean? We eliminate the negatives; we accent and affirm the positives. We express sorrow for hurting others; we repent by striving not to harm them in the future.

In other words, we go beyond the minimum requirement of accepting the gospels and how they tell us to live. (That is, we reject the attitude "Just tell us what we have to do to get just inside the gates of heaven!") Instead, we embrace the actions of Jesus, actions that help us live our life fully—with grace and wisdom. Kingdom living is a search for the extraordinary in ordinary life; kingdom living happens in the midst of this ordinary life.

We began this chapter with the story of an annual family get together—a little slice of life in the kingdom. We're not told what sacrifices the family members made to plan and to get to the gathering. But we know for sure that they had to do a lot to come together. Why come together? Why gather memories like this? To keep our families intact. Doing this is no small accomplishment. However, it is a special kind of kingdom work.

When the family in our story gathers, the older members invite all generations to join in the family fun. The family excludes no one; everyone can play in the game, not just those who are good at it! Let's be clear here: Wrapped in this very simple annual affair are all the realities of what God has promised and given us. God's kingdom *begun* right in the middle of our life.

Morality is the heart-talk that accompanies us in all our walks.

In similar ways, Jesus gathered with those he loved. One of the wonderful scenes after the resurrection is when he cooked fish on an open fire for his friends. If the risen Christ could take time to do something as ordinary as prepare a meal at the side of a lake, family gatherings can be quite important for all of us!

And all this kingdom life is indeed happy. From the standpoint of the kingdom, happiness, goodness, and holiness (blessedness) are all the same. God invites us to live now in the kingdom. God opens the door; we accept the invitation (or don't!); we enter through what we call a conversion—a change of heart.

What happens when we change the direction of our heart? We think and feel differently (like Jesus); we develop a different attitude toward others (once again, we model our attitude on Jesus' attitude); we act differently because we have fallen in love with the actions of Jesus, with Jesus himself.

The heart is a wonderful biblical image signifying that which is deepest in us. Morality is not just a set of rules, laws, or commandments that we must follow and apply to one aspect of life or another. Morality goes much deeper than that. It is the heart-talk that accompanies us in all our walks—from the kitchen to the living room, from the home to the factory or office, from the idea to the action, from God to each of us. Morality is our way of being. And the way we "be" Christians.

> *"By the working of the Word of Christ, we slowly bear fruit in the Church to the glory of God."*
>
> CCC, 1724

Children watch all the time.

Deciding what is right or what is wrong in our daily lives is not easy! Sometimes we don't even go through a process of deciding. Sometimes we just act out of habit, perhaps from the way our parents raised us.

Every single day God invites us to turn toward goodness. Where do we find goodness? In simple things: like letting a car go in front of us, listening yet again to an elderly friend tell a story, calling to see how a distant relative is doing, making a special dessert someone in the family loves, not yelling back at an angry spouse, and on and on and on.

As long as we're awake, these invitations to little goodnesses come. Eventually, they add up to be a representation of who we are. We are known by the way we do this or that in our life. This was true for Jesus. And as people watched him and experienced him as he interacted with others, they recognized that he was unique. The way he acted—toward friends and strangers, the sick, the poor, the alienated, the despised, the lonely, the confused—was different from the way many others of the time acted.

Children watch all the time. As parents, as adults, we share the responsibility for the world of tomorrow and for many more tomorrows. The little persons in the yard next door or in the supermarket aisle or in the classroom or in the pew in front of us or in our hearts and homes are watching. They want to learn from us; we want to teach. Are we teaching then the lessons that lead to goodness and holiness and happiness?

Are you conscious enough of your behavior to know if you are being a good spiritual director? Are the little and big goodnesses obvious in what these children see you do? Children are drawn to light. Is your light shining? The world of darkness needs it.

A Psalm

Shout for joy to God our defender; / sing praise to the God of Jacob! / Start the music and beat the tambourines; / play pleasant music on the harps and the lyres. / Blow the trumpet for the festival, / when the moon is new and when the moon is full. / This is the law in Israel, / an order from the God of Jacob. . . . / "I am the Lord your God, / who brought you out of Egypt. / Open your mouth, and I will feed you."

Psalm 81:1–4, 6-7, 8–10

An Invitation to the Party

We in family know how to put on a party,
Lord Jesus.
We know what's needed, how to organize,
how to entertain,
And we do it for lots of reasons,
Especially to come to be with one another
And thus, to be with you.

Cuz' you, Lord, make it happen;
You make us happy at our own party.
As we nourish our bodies and our souls
In laughter, games, and stuffing mouths
With all you offer.

Because it's all your party, Lord.
We have accepted the invitation,
And we are prepared to prepare ourselves and our children
And our children's children.

We know your party takes work, Lord,
Like any party.
But we'll work, you know that,
We'll live our lives to their absolute fullest,
Accepting all the joy you offer
And surviving the pain.
And all the while getting to know you and yours,
Like we know our own family.
And then someday, Lord,
We'll all be together
For one great family reunion!

Amen.

CHAPTER TWO

Created Both Free and Responsible

"Honey! Grab the fuzz buster from my car!" he yelled from the garage. Then he helped five-year-old Timmy into his car seat and went around to check the oil. He didn't drive the van that often, so he had to do an equipment check.

Their ten-year-old, Melissa, came out the front door and climbed into her usual seat. The only two left were Donna, his wife, and John, their sixteen-year-old.

Once everybody was buckled up, he took the radar detector from his wife's hands, placed it on the dashboard, and started the car.

They had to travel only forty miles to the game, but they wanted to get there in plenty of time because the stands would be loaded with hometown people wanting to see the team play. They had two hours, but with Timmy they usually had to make two to four stops so he could inspect fast-food bathrooms! Once out on the open road, they all began to relax and conversations took shape.

"It's gonna be a nice day for the game," his wife said. "Too bad we didn't plan to leave earlier and stop by Mattie and Tom's."

"Mommy, can I have a cookie yet?" the five-year-old asked. This was a record! They'd made it onto the highway before Timmy demanded something to eat!

Donna passed cookies around, and Jim set his up on the dash instead of in his lap, while he shifted gears. Suddenly, Melissa, the ten-year-old, asked, "Daddy, how come you use one of those things to catch cops?"

He could feel his wife hold her breath, awaiting his answer. This had been an issue with them for a long time, and she hadn't heard an acceptable response yet.

"Well, Honey, it's so we can save time getting to the game," he offered in explanation.

"Huh? I don't know what that means," she answered.

"This thing tells me if there's a policeman up ahead, so I don't get stopped," he tried again.

"And if there were a policeman, why would he stop you?" she pursued.

"If I were going faster than the speed limit. But I'd slow down, so he wouldn't," the father retorted.

"How come you don't just watch the little thing there that shows you the numbers?" she said. "Isn't that what it's for? How come you can go faster than the signs say? If they get us what happens? Will they arrest us? Is it wrong to go too fast? Is it okay to have one of those? How come everybody doesn't?"

At the end of her list of questions, everyone in the car grew still.

"Those who accept my commandments and obey them are the ones who love me. My Father will love those who love me; I too will love them and reveal myself to them.

"Those who love me will obey my teaching. My Father will love them, and my Father and I will come to them and live with them. Those who do not love me do not obey my teaching. And the teaching you have heard is not mine, but comes from the Father, who sent me.

"I have told you this while I am still with you. The Helper, the Holy Spirit, whom the Father will send in my name, will teach you everything and make you remember all that I have told you.

"Peace is what I leave you; it is my own peace that I give you. I do not give it as the world does. Do not be worried and upset; do not be afraid."

John 14:21, 23–27

"Live life as I've shown you."

Jesus gathered with families. Time after time in the Scriptures, we meet him in a home or some other place involved with the family in some of it's ordinary experiences like getting water or having a wedding or funeral or just walking a road (read: driving the car). Ordinary experiences.

In the above scriptural passage, Jesus says that he lives with those families, those persons, who accept his commandments. What does he mean? Two things: (1) He lives in the right feelings and actions of our heart; he loves us; he reveals God to us. (2) Jesus actually moves into our home, into the lives of the person or the family living in our home! That is, Jesus becomes so familiar to us that we feel he is just another member of our family.

What Jesus seems to be saying, with great clarity and simplicity, is "It's simple, folks: live life as I've shown you, and I will be with you forever, and I will give you peace."

Sometimes Jesus asks very important questions through children. Let's think about the family in our opening story. They probably weren't feeling peaceful when silence fell over the car. Feeling peaceful isn't easy when we're trying to cover up what could be a wrong.

The dynamics of this story present us with two questions: (1) Can we use a contemporary high-tech method (a "fuzz buster") for a "good" (avoiding a ticket). (2) Does this attitude coincide with Jesus' message?

Being warned that a caregiver of the road (a patrol officer) is somewhere up ahead does not remove the fact that the driver is breaking a speeding law and may possibly even be jeopardizing the safety of himself and others. But perhaps the greater wrong is the message he is giving his children. In effect, he's saying, "It's okay to do something wrong, kids, as long as we don't get caught!" Hmmmmm. Doesn't sound much like Jesus.

The children, who often see much more clearly than we do, probably know innately that something doesn't fit right in their father's logic. The parents' responsibility to live and model good, honest, behavior is in jeopardy here.

We face these moral dilemmas all the time. Choosing the good or the not-so-good is both a freedom and a responsibility. And Jesus quietly waits.

God gifts us with freedom so that we can choose to love.

The world has witnessed some incredible political events in recent times. For instance, literally millions of people enslaved by totalitarian governments gained their political freedom almost overnight. Played out before the rest of the world through the miracle of television, the joy of the liberated people was obvious.

With the restrictions lifted, the people of these countries could travel freely and could be much more in charge of their own lives. For many, the opening of the churches in these countries was the greatest symbol of the deeper meaning of their new freedoms.

For Catholics in the small yet mighty country of Lithuania, the departure of the Russian troops from their soil seemed like the second coming of Christ. Their churches, after being boarded up or turned into state museums for decades, were now opened. The people poured in to give thanks to God. They were free, totally free to be who they were—devoted and faithful Catholics. Their joyous "Alleluias" spread throughout the hills surrounding Vilnius, their capital city.

Of course, we don't need to be Catholics to appreciate the value of political and religious freedom. Wanting to be free has something to do with our human nature. We are born with a hunger both for both political and personal freedom. We want to be able to say yes or no, stop or go. And we all want to be able to say it for ourselves. We abhor slavery of any kind. Freedom is our right because of our human dignity, a dignity that goes back to our origin in God.

Freedom allows us choice. We can decide to be one thing or another, to do one thing or another. The greater our sense of personal freedom, the more options we have.

We can, as we all know, just go along with the crowd. We can become creatures of habit. Then we neither think about nor deliberate over what we can do. We just "do." Automatic pilot. Cruise control. Thus we let our personal freedom lie dormant within us—unused, wasted, trashed.

Part of the role of family is to encourage the use of personal freedom. But how can that be? Isn't family supposed to develop good habits, teach the important rules of life, and see that children follow them?

Yes, that's true, for some things, especially those areas of life in which children, even teens, might be hurt. Then freedom may not be as important as survival. Nevertheless, because our family is the school of love, we must also be the school of freedom. And that means that we learn how to use our freedom—our free choices—for the good of the universe.

The power of freedom

God gives us that kind of power.

Freedom sets choices before us. Weighing each choice, we eventually select one over the other(s). And from that choice, the rest of our life unravels.

We all know exactly what that's like. We can reflect back on our own personal journey when we decided to go to a high school dance or game. At the event we met the person who eventually became our marriage partner.

Or we decided to go to college or join the military or go right to work after high school and our decision affected everything thereafter. Our personal decisions affect us as well as the lives of others, especially in our family. Why? Because, as family we are a group of individuals who make a whole.

Other decisions—economic, work-related—affect our families too. For example, on our fortieth birthday, we decide to start a business that manufactures a sophisticated gyroscope system for flight. The factory provides a living for many families. And as they spend the money they earn, other families get jobs and help other people. Then the gyroscope saves an airplane from a crash that would have taken the lives of hundreds! One decision—build a factory—affects hundreds, thousands, millions of people!

But that decision goes farther back than our fortieth birthday. Back where? To the responsible parents who decided they wanted one more child. That child became the builder of the factory, which made the gyroscopes, which saved the plane in the storm and brought home an individual who eventually perhaps found a cure for cancer!

When we evaluate new situations in our lives and make free decisions, we make things happen. And as our world changes, we change. This leads to still more decisions and actions and results of the decisions. Our decision making has endless ramifications—some good, some bad.

Of course, we can never foresee all the ramifications of a free decision, but we know they are many. And part of our use of freedom, as God intends, is to take into account what might happen as a result of making this or that decision.

Before we make a decision, we factor into our calculations something about the possible results of one or another possibility. When we make our decisions with good in our mind and in our heart, then we aim for good results; we avoid results that might be evil or harmful. Our decisions become actions; our actions produce results; the results change the world—for better or for worse. God gives us that kind of power.

Freedom and responsibility

Do you want spinach or squash?

Freedom does not stand alone. It spreads out through the other decisions made after it. In making a free decision, we invest ourselves in the decision; we express who we are; we express our values and the goodness or evil that may be a part of our identity. Through our decisions, we respond to what we face in our life and in ourselves.

Our free decisions echo back to us and reform us and the world anew. Philosophers called existentialists wrote about freedom in the early part of the twentieth century. Acutely aware of the massive social changes in society, they realized what the impact of mass media, mass industrialization, and mass centralization on society would be.

And what did these thinkers fear more than anything else? The loss of freedom. They feared that the system (big government, big business, big church, whatever) would decide for us. Thus, we would have no freedom to choose; the system ("Big Brother") would choose for us.

These philosophers called for awareness of this dangerous reversal. They praised the importance of being free and making decisions. Many existentialists did not particularly care whether our decisions were moral or not; that was not their issue. They just wanted us to affirm our rightful dignity as free persons and to act accordingly.

Yet, to provide the full picture, we also need to attend to the consequences of our decisions. We do this by making reasonable or plausible estimates about what will happen. We weigh the consequences. If we don't do this, we invite deep trouble, and sometimes the effects are irreversible. Of course, no one knows for sure what will happen as a result of a particular choice, but if we've been given the freedom to choose and if we learn from our mistakes, we can be good guessers.

We help our children to become good guessers by providing them—early on—with choices. We start with small things like—Do you want spinach or squash with your chicken? Later we provide choices that have to do with friends or places to go.

The gift of freedom

The gift of freedom is connected with our capacity to love. Love is not just attraction to someone or something. It is one's free choice of another; it is the establishment of a very special kind of relationship—one of closeness. As Saint Thomas Aquinas, the great Catholic theologian, wrote, love is a treasured relationship in which we value another simply for the sake of the other.

God takes a great chance in creating freedom.

God gifts us with freedom so that we can choose to love or not to love God. In other words, we can choose to reject God's love. God takes a great chance in creating freedom and placing it within us. We can say "Yes!" to all God offers and asks of us and that's wonderful—both for us and for God. Or we can say "No!" and that is tragic for both of us too.

When we use our freedom for good (which primarily means loving God and loving each other), we receive the results of goodness—eternal life in God, who is Goodness, Holiness, Love, overflowing. The determination of whether we spend our eternity in Love rests with us and with our use of the gift of freedom. Do we choose the good? That is, do we serve and love others in the way Jesus showed us? Or do we choose evil? Do we choose those free actions that bring hurt and misery and pain and stunted growth to others—and to ourselves?

Obviously God creates freedom because of the wondrous good that can come from its use. As we reflect on the challenges of the Christian life, let's consider the good that can come from our choices. Living a morally good life is serious business. Especially for ourselves.

We have the power, rooted in our freedom, to accept or reject the love God offers us so joyfully. We have the power to respond with love or to reject with bitterness and malice. And we make this choice from moment to moment in our lives. We have the capacity to do so much good, to give so much love! Our ability to love tenderly, to act justly, to walk humbly before God is almost beyond our imagination. Yet, real.

"Freedom is exercised in relationships between human beings. Every human person, created in the image of God, has the natural right to be recognized as a free and responsible being. All owe to each other this duty of respect. The right to the exercise of freedom . . . *is an inalienable requirement of the dignity of the human person."*

CCC, 1738

Everything we do has ramifications.

Because we are not isolated individuals living in a mountain cave or a hermitage, we have power over other people. That is, with our freedom to make decisions, we affect the lives of others.We make many decisions, simple ones, like deciding what to fix for dinner (which affects everyone who eats it) and more complex ones, like deciding to knock off from work and lie to the boss (which probably makes our co-workers' tasks more difficult).

When we throw a rock into a lake, we see rings and rings of ever-widening circles. So it is with our actions. No big deal, we might say about a particular choice. But in our life, the size of the "rock" (our decision/choice) and where we "throw" it (our actions) might have great consequences. We all know that we can make "bad" decisions that deeply hurt others. Thus, being free to choose is an awesome responsibility.

We adults make far-reaching decisions every day, and if we are parents, the other persons in our families are watching. When our decision causes grave pain to our children, horrible effects can follow. For example, we may become involved with someone outside our marriage, refuse help and deny the possibility of change within the old relationship, and decide to walk away from our marriage. This decision changes our family forever, and it forever touches the lives of our children and *our children's children.*

Sometimes we make selfish decisions. When we do this, we seldom consider the pain inflicted on our family and the example we are setting for children, our friends, and anyone who knows or loves our family. Such a decision, conceived in selfishness and executed in thoughtlessness, generates tremendous power over the lives of all born into the family in the future.

Yet sometimes we use a good decision-making process when we make choices like the above. We seek help; we do serious work to better our relationship; we identify problems and changes needed. But if, for whatever reason, our relationship still doesn't work; we may have no hope for it. Then, through help, we may agree to end our marriage because an ending to the pain is the only solution.

Just as we made a decision to marry, now we make a decision to unmarry. And throughout the process, we keep foremost in our hearts and minds the fact that our decision affects our children. For them we will learn to co-parent fairly and justly, despite the fact that we no longer love one another. If we can do this, our decision, our free choice, will probably result in good healthy relationships later—both for us and for our children and our children's children.

We've all made some far-reaching decision. Perhaps it was similar to the example above. Looking back on this decision, we sometimes have a totally different view from when we first began to make our choice. (It's like following a certain path in the woods and suddenly turning around and seeing where we just came from. The view back over our shoulder seems completely different from the view we had when we started forward.)

As you look back at a decision, do you see anything you would now do differently? If so, can you forgive yourself for the mistake you made? God understands; God forgives; God longs for you to forgive yourself. Perhaps, then, you can.

And if your decision affected others, do you need to ask for their forgiveness? Have you asked them to forgive you?

Asking for forgiveness is a good thing because being free of the pain of guilt is wonderful!

God gives us the gift of freedom at all times during our life. We hear of conversions to God at the time of death. We know too of people who have dedicated themselves to God at a very early age. God's time is all the time and so is the possibility of freedom. In other words, in freedom we can change the course of our lives most any time.

But it is also part of modern life that people are creatures of habit. While we might make free decisions, we appear not to. Day after day, year after year, we keep goin' but seemingly not goin' anywhere. All this points out that freedom while available, still has to be received. It has to be brought into our lives. And, as strange as it sounds, that can be scary. Maybe because it is always tied to responsibility. Maybe it's because we are fearful. Maybe we just plain forget and have to begin to remember to exercise this freedom.

A Psalm

Be good to me your servant,
so that I may live and obey your teachings.
Open my eyes, so that I may see
the wonderful truths in your law.
I am here on earth for just a little while;
do not hide your commands from me.
Psalm 119:17–19

In the Blink of an Eye

od, you live only in this moment,
An eternal moment.
But if we live to be seventy or eighty
or ninety,
We think that we've been here on earth a long,
long time.
But heaven has no clocks,
No calendars,
No turn of the century
Or the millennium,
No history.
We can't even imagine what heaven will be like
Especially without age,
Or aging each day.

All we can do is just get up every morning,
Welcoming a brand-new day,
And live that day to its fullest
In caring and loving those precious people
Who happen to be here on this earth
At the same time we are.

And then someday, hopefully,
After doing this,
We'll wake up one day in heaven with you.
And never have to say good-bye to another day.
Perhaps even tomorrow!

Amen.

CHAPTER THREE

Images of God in Flesh and Spirit

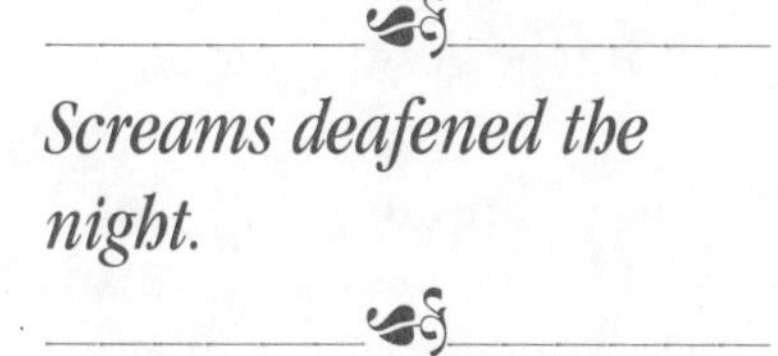

Finally! His two-year-old son was asleep again. The tired father gently slipped his forearm out from under Jonathan's head, moved the child's soft body onto the couch, and curled his own body off the couch.

"Best to leave him here," the father thought. "If I move him, those teeth are going to start acting up again, and we'll be at it again!"

He carefully placed the new coat that belonged to his daughter, Trish, over the baby. He gazed at the sleeping face for a moment. So peaceful now. Then he turned toward the kitchen to get a glass of milk.

The silence exploded!

He thought the house had blown up because he ended up on the floor in the kitchen, just steps away from the living room.

He whirled in panic to defend himself against the unknown. Screams deafened the night!

Later, he remembered that his wife, Gina, was already in the living room when he got back in there.

It was she who screamed.

And he remembered that she hysterically threw herself to the floor and thrashed around.

And, "God, oh God!" he remembered seeing his dying child!

Blood everywhere. No chance for Jonathan to even wake up and cry out for his parents! No chance to shield the baby's soft body with his own. No chance to move him to safety, to throw his little sleeping body to safety.

No chance! No chance! No chance!

"Oh God!"

And he remembered seeing Trish's coat and, in his pain, thinking, "How awful! We'll never get the blood off her coat!"

"A drive-by killing took the life of an innocent two-year-old today," the voice on the TV said.

The words wounded him. *An innocent two-year-old!* His dead son had become a statistic—a cold, impersonal, uncaring statistic! "They've labeled him!" he cried out in grief and sank down on the couch.

"Oh God, help us! My baby is dead. My sleeping son is dead! He never had a chance to live! To feel the sand at the beach . . . the experience of a baseball game . . . his first kiss! a child of his own!" the father's shoulder shook as he cried into his hands.

"My God! Our children are killing one another!"

After they had left, an angel of the Lord appeared in a dream to Joseph and said: "Herod will be looking for the child in order to kill him. So get up, take the child and his mother and escape to Egypt, and stay there until I tell you to leave!"

When Herod realized that the visitors from the East had tricked him, he was furious. He gave orders to kill all the boys in Bethlehem and its neighborhood who were two years old and younger—he had learned from the visitors about the time when the star had appeared.

Matthew 2:13, 16

The first martyrs of the church.

Unfortunately, since the beginning of time, we humans have been killing our children. The above story is one of the most heart-wrenching passages from Scripture. We read it during the Christmas season, a time of joy in which the church recounts the story of Jesus' birth.

The writer of the gospel tells us that Herod attempted to kill Jesus, the child, before he could grow up and threaten Herod's kingdom. (Herod thought that the birth of a new "king" meant literally an earthly king.) To be sure and find the right child, Herod killed all baby boys under two years of age in Bethlehem.

From time to time, the movies have depicted that slaughter with terrible realism: Troops storm into houses and snatch the babies from the arms of their mothers or fathers; the military pursue parents who try to escape with their little ones; callous soldiers brutally massacre all the boy babies they can find. We call this narrative the "the slaughter of the Holy Innocents." These babies were the first martyrs of the church. They gave their lives, so to speak, for the sake of Jesus.

Our own holy innocents are still dying—in terrible ways—*all over the world.* The evil in a world that deprives innocent children of a future seems to be getting worse. And even more tragically, our children are killing one another!

The phrase *a drive-by* was not even in our vocabulary ten years ago. Now we use the words all the time. At first, the accidental shooting of noninvolved children shocked us beyond belief; now these incidents are so common in some areas of our country that we barely blink an eye when we read about the death of another child. Yet families, like the one in our opening story, are forever changed by the pain, the grief, the senselessness.

As are we all. For we are all part of the same body—the Body of Christ Jesus. We are sisters and brothers, mothers, fathers, uncles, aunts, grandparents, and cousins of one another. The English poet John Donne once wrote, "Never send to know for whom the bell tolls; it tolls for thee." He knew, as do we, that we are all connected; what affects one of us, affects all.

Any child killed is our child killed. Any adult raped or otherwise brutally injured is our body being mutilated. We are all part of one another; we belong to one another, created one and all by the same God for the same reasons. Being created in the image and likeness of God, bearing the flesh Jesus bore, living in the Spirit, unites us all. What happens to one of us, happens to each of us. And as we care for one another—as we love and serve and cherish—so we care for our God.

The reality of evil present in our world victimizes the family in our opening story. But we cannot chalk up yet another child to being in the wrong place at the wrong time. Nor can we continue to condone any other child's death by blaming someone or something else. Sometimes not doing anything is in itself a decision to do wrong.

Life! Precious life.

What is happening in our world—senseless and malicious killing—horrifies us. We are bothered so deeply because we know what could be. We know God's original dream for all of us. Something has gone wrong.

God creates us as free individuals. We are free to do good and to avoid evil. Of course, the reality of evil in our world is as mysterious as is the reality of goodness.

As far as we know, humans are the only creatures who can actually violate their own natures. A lion cannot act in an unlionish way. Nor can a robin sing like a lark. But we humans have the uncanny ability to violate ourselves—in an inhuman way. Freedom allows us to act against who we are.

God virtues

Think of faith more as a verb than a noun.

The word *virtue* comes from a Latin word meaning "power" or "strength." A person of virtue can stand up against the evil tendencies in our world, against those tugs toward evil we experience in ourselves and others.

Our church gives special attention to three very strong virtues that come from God. The theological virtues are faith, hope and love, which we sometimes call charity. These virtues connect us with God; they enable us believe God, trust God, and love God.

Faith means that we listen to God and accept whatever God communicates to us. Sometimes we cannot understand all of what God reveals nor why, but we still accept the message and the messenger—God's Spirit in us. Sometimes God communicates to us through other individuals and through the community of believers.

A faithful person is open, receptive, and ready to connect with truth all the time because faith is an active virtue. In fact, think of faith more as a verb than a noun. Faith keeps us moving ahead on our journey to the fulfillment of our hunger for God. Faith keeps us seeking and searching for the truth of our relationship to God, to ourselves, to our family members, our friends, our global community. Faith is not only the acceptance of a dogma of the church. No. It is also a holding fast to God. Families know the difference between a value in their lives that is heart-felt and one that is not.

Hope is a wonderful virtue that we often sidestep. Hope is the courage to go on in spite of difficulties. When we hope, we walk through an open door and trust that something, not a void, exists beyond the opening.

Hope is truly the virtue of the strong. It is not simply optimism, which often closes our eyes to reality. No. Hope is open-eyed; it sees the evil in organizations and people; it sees failure and disappointment. But it still continues on the path to goodness and love. Families thrive on hope—hope for a child to get into a certain school, or do better in school, or stay in school. Hope for a better day than yesterday. Hope for relief from our many worries. Every day we get up and start hoping all over again.

When we love, we image God in the best possible way.

We need to place our hope and confidence not in the way we do things or in seemingly powerful organizations. Instead of these finite receptacles of hope, we place our hope in the abiding love of our compassionate God. Then evil or weakness will not drag us down and we can stay strong in the face of adversity. We trust God's promise that the will and the ways of God will prevail. Maybe not today or tomorrow, but in the end, God's love *will* triumph.

In his letters to the early Christian communities, Saint Paul says that love (charity) is the greatest of these three virtues. Why? It connects us with our God and with everyone else. Love is the primary energy of human life. When we love, we image God in the best possible way. One of the inspired sections of the Christian Testament is Paul's first letter to the community of believers at Corinth. Paul says,

> Love is patient and kind; it is not jealous or conceited or proud; love is not ill-mannered or selfish or irritable; love does not keep a record of wrongs; love is not happy with evil, but is happy with the truth. Love never gives up; and its faith, hope, and patience never fail.
>
> *1 Corinthians 13:4–7*

As we reflect on these words, we see them not only as a way to love others but also as the way God loves us. When we read them in the light of God's love for us, we find that our faith and hope and love grow by leaps and bounds. For who of us could fail to become good and holy when loved in that way?

Love is the primary virtue of God-inspired relationships. When we love we create a positive space between ourselves. We fill this space with care and service because love wills life, not death. That's why reports of murder and violence between people offend us. These actions violate the God within us; they violate the image of God in the murderer and in the murdered.

How we relate to each other eventually becomes the most meaningful sign of the presence of the kingdom of God. The kingdom grows into God's vision when we respond lovingly to the homeless stranger, the hopeless worker, the hungry child. In these relationships, in the love we share with others, we find God and we deepen within ourselves the image of the God who created us.

God created us as individuals, but God means for us to work, play, love, and pray together as equal partners. As we live together as equals, we reflect the life and the love of the Triune God—the Father, Son, and Holy Spirit. God is love itself—deep, eternal, overflowing, creating, seeking us out moment by moment. When we love, God lives in us in a special way. Thus, love is one of the most precious human virtues.

Passion and emotions

God looked at us, smiled, and said, "Nice job!"

Passion is a word that seems to escape a clear definition. Primarily because it is both an emotion as well as a drive and conviction about something. Most often we say someone acts with passion. We also use the word to refer to the experience of Jesus' suffering—his passion. This reminds us that he entered into his last days with feelings and convictions.

Many Catholics assume that the church is always on the side of being quiet, serene, placid—passionless. Despite our assumption, however, the church values passion as part of our emotions and as an important part of human life, including the Christian life. God made us both passionate and emotional so as to assist us in our movement toward good.

All our created gifts (like passion) come right out of that huge blueprint God used in creating us. No part of our body, our mind, or our spirit is evil. God looked at us (as a whole and in all our parts), smiled, and said, "Nice job! Good work! These are definitely keepers!"

Yet we are also familiar with the phrase "being carried away by one's emotions." That describes us when we operate only out of our emotional state. And that's dangerous. Why? Because only one part of us is active.

However, when we set emotions or passion aside and use only our minds we tread on dangerous waters too. We need to act wholly—using both mind and passion. We can be too much "head" just as we can be too much "feelings." But we probably cannot be too much heart because love knows no limits!

Passion and emotions are good. They power us for moving from stop to start, from separation to connecting, as we journey toward the good who is God.

Sin and separation

Sin is a deep-down refusal to love—even ourselves.

We know a dark side exists in our human life. It comes from our freedom and takes the form of denying the image of God in which we are made. It is a deep-down refusal to love God and each other—even ourselves. We call this refusal sin. When we sin, we turn our hearts away from God toward a way of being contrary to God's way.

And further, when we reject God in a total and complete way, we call this mortal sin. The word *mortal* is from the Latin word *mors,* meaning death. Mortal sin destroys the life of God in us.

The church has been clear on all that is required for us to commit a mortal sin:

(1) We have to do something grave. We have to do something that is absolutely contrary to the will and love of our compassionate God. Serious sin is connected with a serious human action. Mortal sins are acts of wanton destructiveness. Taking innocent human life, as in our opening story, is the kind of harmful act that could be a mortal sin.

(2) We must know that what we are doing is, in fact, a serious matter. It must cause serious destruction or evil and we must be aware of that fact.

(3) We must give sufficient deliberation or thought to what we are about to do, and we must consent (freely and without external pressure) to the act. We can commit a mortal sin only when we act with knowledge and freedom.

What our tradition labels as venial sin is connected with less serious matter. Rather than disconnecting us from our relationship with God, venial sin weakens it. We become less able to recognize the presence of God in our life, in ourselves, and in one another. We become less able to practice the three great virtues of faith, hope, and love. We grow dull in our understanding of God's love and will.

Let's be real here. All sin—mortal and venial—is harmful to us, to our neighbor, and in a sense, to our God. Whenever we commit a moral evil (a sin), whether its mortal or venial, we are all the less for it. We all suffer. Why? Because we are all a part of one another. God has created us to be a family and what one family member does affects all family members.

Sin is very real. We all sin. And so we all need the generous, forgiving love of our God; we all need the saving grace of Jesus. Daily, we give thanks for our certain knowledge (a gift of faith) that our God always forgives. In truth, our God longs to forgive; hungers for us; waits patiently for ever and a day for us to want to rid ourselves of the evil of sin.

Our life is a drama in which good and evil struggle. Waiting in the wings and hovering over us is a good that far surpasses our imagination. God's love waits for us even in our sin. We may separate ourselves from God, but God stays close, always inviting our return, even longing for it.

When we choose the good we affect both ourselves and others. In fact, our goodness can spread throughout the world. That's great news. But there is other news, too, and its the kind that more easily finds its way to our newspaper and news broadcasts. It is the news of human evil and sin. Like the murder of the baby in our opening story. We believe, however, because the Scriptures assure us of this—that good always conquers evil.

A twenty-four hour job.

Love has a real connection with correction, at least for those of us who care for children. *Correction* is an interesting word. It implies that there is indeed something which warrants correcting. For example, if a child is acting out in a store, screaming and yelling for something which the parent is not giving, the parent may want to "correct' that behavior.

Some parents correct by yelling back and slapping or threatening. Still others gently bend down to the child's level and, with loving hands holding the child in direct view, speak clearly to the child, explaining why the child will not get the desired yummy or toy. Then they remove the child from the store if he or she does not comply. One parent reacts; the other responds.

The difference in the correction is in what the child learns. Scream and yell and slap, or talk out the problem and learn limits. *Correct*-tion can in itself be good or not so good. It can be correct or not.

Teaching children right and wrong is a twenty-four-hour job. So much challenges us. So much in our world invites our children to act in another way. For example, many Saturday morning television programs encourage violence and the acquiring of more and more stuff!

God put in us a desire to seek good, to want good, to feel good about good.

We need good feelings about ourselves and so do our children. And their good behavior deserves appropriate praise. Parents accustomed to slapping and scolding can change that approach. They can begin to praise and encourage. We accentuate the positive to eliminate the negative!

Teaching moral behavior begins and continues at home; we know that. We know that children learn limits and acceptable behaviors toward other people at a very early age. And children learn not only by what we say they must do, but also by what they watch *us* do! Good solid acceptable, caring behavior begins with good, acceptable, caring adult behavior. Sadly children sometimes fail to hear our words because our own behavior shouts the opposite to them.

Our faith has carried through the centuries a wonderful word describing the connections between us. It is the word "witness." Most of us know this word as it applies to a court of law. One stands in public before others and "witnesses" to the truth.

But the word has another meaning which stretches to the very origins of Christianity. It refers to the public expression of one's faith in God. And to make that expression in the midst of a community hostile to the faith could cost one's life. The word "witness" is the same word as "martyr."

As we reflect on the influence parents have on children—and the influence children have on parents—and on the influence we all have on each other, we begin to appreciate the power of witnessing.

Part of the strength in being human is the capacity of vulnerability. This same capacity can also be our weakness. We can enjoy and be grateful for the influence we have on each other. We can also be its victim.

Human life is so precious and so precarious. We each carry within us so much power—more than we often realize.

Think about the last time you were with a two- or three-month-old child. Did you find yourself talking gently to him or her, perhaps poking the chubby little chin or cheek and then making some sort of nonsensical human noise to encourage a response?

Children listen and watch you, then they do. If you talk gently to the baby, the baby will grin back at you. If you yell and curse and threaten, the child will cringe and cower in fear. What chance is there to grow into a loving human being? What chance to believe in a loving God?

Love begets love; hatred begets hatred; abuse begets a child who feels no security. You reap what you sow: you find what you look for. You can coo or curse or you can love. From each of these actions, children will learn something. The question is what do you want them to learn?

"God has not willed to reserve to himself all exercise of power. He entrusts to every creature the functions it is capable of performing, according to the capacities of its own nature. This mode of governance ought to be followed in social life. The way God acts in governing the world, which bears witness to such great regard for human freedom, should inspire the wisdom of those who govern human communities. They should behave as ministers of divine providence."

CCC, 1884

A Psalm

How happy are those whose strength comes from you,
who are eager to make the pilgrimage to Mount Zion.
As they pass through the dry valley of Baca,
it becomes a place of springs;
the autumn rain fills it with pools.
They grow stronger as they go;
they will see the God of gods on Zion.

Psalm 84:5–7

One Family

e are only one, dear God, but we are one.
And sometimes we have a hard time
Just being us.
Cuz' there's so much we have to do just to live
Day in and day out.

But we can do something,
Because, as members of your family here on earth,
We belong to one another.
We know others are in great need
And great pain
And we can do something.
What we can do,
We must do,
And by your grace, we will do.
Amen.

CHAPTER FOUR

God's Direction in Us—The Voice of Conscience

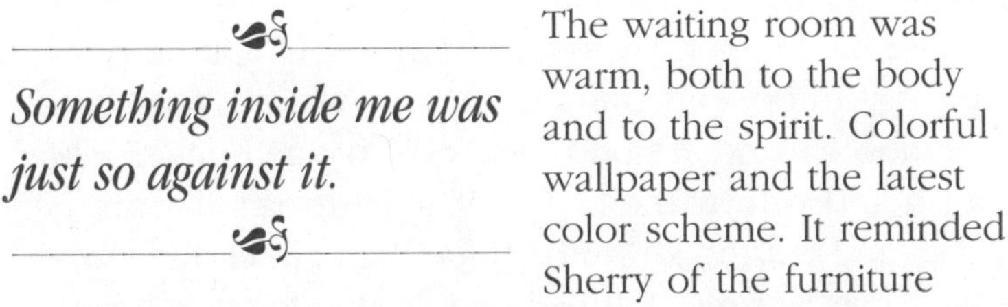

Something inside me was just so against it.

The waiting room was warm, both to the body and to the spirit. Colorful wallpaper and the latest color scheme. It reminded Sherry of the furniture section of the store she worked in, a real designer room.

Sherry gave her name to the receptionist and sat down to wait. The lawyer had been referred to her by a friend at school and was supposed to be both understanding and good. And that's what Sherry needed—someone to handle the adoption, someone who understood the issues involved, but who would also find a good home for the baby.

Tears welled up in the young woman's eyes again. In a minute or two she'd be fine. It happened all the time now that she was further along. Pretty soon she'd be showing, and then she'd probably cry a lot more!

The receptionist welcomed her into the inner offices, and she followed her to a door at the far end. A young, stylish woman came around from the desk to greet her, and Sherry immediately liked her.

After a few moments of quiet chitchat, they quickly got into particulars. Soon an hour had passed, and she'd poured out her whole story. Even the part about getting an abortion.

"I . . . I couldn't do it, you know? I had the appointment and everything. Something inside me was just so against it. In my head I knew that God would forgive me and everything, because I had to think of me first, right? I mean, God says we have to love ourselves first in order to love somebody else. Well, I thought it was okay. And it was, I mean, people do it thousands of times a day."

She stopped and took a deep breath. Then she continued. "But I just couldn't do it, you know. My heart felt like hamburger. I was all chewed up about it. And I felt that to do something so serious when I was in that condition was not a good idea. So I backed out. Took a long ride down by the beach. Watched seagulls and the waves and felt the air. And suddenly it struck me. This wasn't my decision. I already made my decision when Peter and I got sexually involved."

She paused for a moment, glanced around the room at the pictures and the plants and then turned once again to the woman who was listening so patiently and reassuringly.

"This baby was God's idea. And if I goofed that up, who knows what would happen to me? I just know I couldn't live with it. The decision, that is. And I couldn't live with a baby either. But, in that salt air, no way was I gonna take away that baby's chance to see and feel the beach. I just couldn't do it. And I'm glad. Now. Scared spitless, yes. But glad!" Her lip quivered yet a smile came directed at the woman sitting beside her.

Then Sherry looked deep into the woman's eyes and said, "You will help me, won't you? This baby deserves a good chance at the life I've given it. Okay?"

The other woman just looked at her, gently smiling. Then she leaned forward and said, "Of course. That's my job. But I'll do it for another reason, and that's because this baby is so lucky to have you for its birth mom."

It was winter, and the Festival of the Dedication of the Temple was being celebrated in Jerusalem. Jesus was walking in Solomon's Porch in the Temple, when the people gathered around him and asked, "How long are you going to keep us in suspense? Tell us the plain truth: are you the Messiah?"

Jesus answered, "I have already told you, but you would not believe me. The deeds I do by my Father's authority speak on my behalf; but you will not believe, for you are not my sheep. My sheep listen to my voice; I know them, and they follow me. I give them eternal life, and they shall never die. No one can snatch them away from me. What my Father has given me is greater than everything, and no one can snatch them away from the Father's care. The Father and I are one.

John 10:22–30

What Jesus would think or say or do.

Jesus lived his life differently from those around him. He broke all kinds of rules on which his culture insisted. For instance, he ate with what some in our time label the "low life"—tax collectors, prostitutes, beggars, the homeless, lepers, the poor. And when he behaved a certain way, his followers asked questions. They wanted him to explain things to them.

In his explanations, Jesus used the world around him—the world he could see as they ambled down the dusty roads of Galilee or sailed across its lake or walked the streets of Jerusalem with its dark streets and its animals being herded to the Temple and its booths filled with trinkets for busy tourists. Jesus talked about planting seeds, fishing, tending the vineyards, lighting a light, and shepherding sheep.

Being compared to sheep was not a put-down for his listeners. On the contrary, they could easily relate to caring for their sheep, especially keeping track of them and not losing any. And they could relate to the fact that their sheep would get to know them and that they would come to know each and every sheep.

So the analogy about following Jesus was a very good one. Obviously, following his voice meant far more than literally walking down the road with him. It meant listening to his words, seeing how he treated others, and then following his example.

Following this voice is easy to do. We simply seek and find the person of Jesus and all he is invites us to do. And when we know (truly know!) what Jesus would think or say or do in a particular instance in our lives, then the voice becomes an internal voice—our conscience.

But there's a catch here. We can hear a voice deep within us that we may think is the voice of conscience, but it can fool us. It can be another voice, calling us to do the opposite of that which Jesus would do.

So the test is always to have what we call an "informed conscience." That is, we come to know Jesus so well that when we act we are sure of what Jesus would do. (Later in this chapter, we'll talk about this some more.)

The young woman in our opening story had obviously made some tough decisions. From her actions, we are led to believe she has indeed followed Jesus' teaching to reverence life. For now, she loves enough to care more about her child's welfare than her own.

Her decision has had grave ramifications for herself, possibly for the child's birth father, and certainly for her family and friends. Yet, to welcome new life and give that new life to his or her eventual adoptive family, this young woman is willing to withstand the scourging, to walk the passion with Jesus.

The voice within her echoes good over evil—the voice of our God.

God made us to enjoy life.

All of us are born into this world with strengths and limitations. Since we are the result of God's best effort at creating, we are even given some of God's own powers. And among the greatest of what God gives us is the gift of freedom. Resting deep within us is the power of choice.

True, many factors can limit our freedom. They can come from ourselves or others. Our physical or psychological needs can overwhelm us if we allow them to. We can, in fact, become slaves of certain needs.

For example, we can "need" to escape the present demands of life through drugs or alcohol. We can allow the need for the ecstatic high of gambling, with its promise of the big hit, to lead us to ruin. We can become so protective of ourselves and our need to feel safe and secure that we never risk ourselves with anyone or anything. We can hide from life. Is this what God wants for us? No.

God wants the very best for each of us. God made us to know; therefore, God wants us to know as much as we can. God made us to enjoy life with all its beauty; therefore, God wants us to experience beauty as much as we can. And most of all, God made us to love; therefore, God wants us to love as much as we can.

To direct us to these wonderful moments, these most fulfilling experiences of knowing and enjoying and loving, God plants within each of us a voice to assist us in making the best possible choices. God does not leave us without help and guidance in deciding what's best.

Why does God help us? Why does God not simply sit on the sidelines—silent, sullen—watching us stumble through the game? Because God wants us to find the good, which is God. God calls us to live and to love wholly, fully. The voice God gives each of us is the voice of the one who loves us more than anyone else, the voice of God.

Simply put, God's voice calls us, without ceasing, to become the incredible human being God created. A one of a kind being; a unique, beautiful creation; a masterpiece beyond price. God invites us to be artists who fashion ourselves, with God's help, into the goodness and beauty that reflects the love of our God. How do we do this? We follow the voice of our conscience—God's voice calling us to wholeness and holiness.

Hearing the voice of God within is not as unusual as it may first sound. The pregnant woman in our opening story eventually recognized that voice within herself. And she knew the voice was the gentle whisper of her God. This voice valued life and valued her. And she followed where it led.

The formation of conscience

It's under our skin, in our bones.

God gives us our conscience at the beginning of life, but this voice needs development. Like virtually everything else in life, our conscience has to learn. In traditional language, it must be informed. An uninformed conscience can be a dangerous companion. It may not see the whole picture. And part of our responsibility in having a conscience is to be sure that it operates with human and Christian wisdom, common sense and street smarts.

The learning process begins, of course, in our family. Every family has its unique slant on reality. Families inherit both customs and a culture, but they also enhance these through the experience of being family. New babies and newly adopted children enter an environment in which a lot is going on.

Within our families we have hundreds of rules about what's right and what's wrong. Through our words and actions, we teach our children attitudes about neighbors;

about people who are of a different race or ethnic background; about politicians, movie stars, and even the clergy. Newborn members come into our family and soak up our attitudes like a dry sponge.

Those of us who are parents are the first to communicate the Gospel to our children. The church calls us the first evangelizers. Of course, our "sermon" is not so much in what we say—but rather, what we do.

We parents communicate the good news of God's love for each of us through the way we look at our children, the way we touch and hold them, the way we speak to them. And we preach the message twenty-four hours a day. This process continues until the death of the last family member (which will happen only at the end of time!). In other words, there is a beginning, but no end to the lessons we teach. Such is the nature of the communication of our faith. Through the gestures of our family's love and forgiveness, our children come to grasp the heart of the Gospel—the good news that God loves us and is with us.

Our families have a lot of power and influence. But the power is incredibly subtle; we hardly notice it. People sometimes leave home thinking that they can leave the influence of family by placing miles between themselves and the family home. Wrong. Family goes along with the traveler because family is part of all of us. It's under our skin, in our bones, our nose, our minds, even in our hearts! We can't cut it out of us.

And if we have influenced our children for the worse, they will suffer for it. Always? Ever? No, not if we recognize that we can change. For example, our family may harbor very negative feelings and judgments about a particular group of people; our family prejudice can be very powerful and persuasive.

But through direct interpersonal encounter with a member of the group we disdain, we—and our children—can change our attitudes. We can learn that "they" are, in fact, good people. Our encounter with this one person of the group we scorned can teach us that "they" are not less than we are. No, they, too, are people whom God loves and cherishes.

Our conscience can grow and change too. But we must want it to change. Another person cannot force us to change; we have to decide that change is for our better. Here is where the role of learning about our faith, especially about Jesus, becomes so important. Each of us has a responsibility to overcome ignorance. Ignorance may seem to be bliss under some circumstances, but being uninformed is never a virtue. Therefore, families, besides being containers of love, must also be centers of learning.

The spirit of inquiry, of curiosity, and of a desire to learn is more often caught than taught. Conversations in front of the television, around the dinner table, and in the car alert the younger members of our families to the real values we cherish. And if we appreciate and encourage new learning, then we truly bless our children! For example, when we watch television with our children, we have a great opportunity to comment openly about our family's Christian values versus the world's values.

And just as learning can be a lifelong endeavor, so, too, is the formative process for our conscience. At its root, conscience is the voice of God within. Conscience is the abiding presence of Jesus, who continues to teach us as he did his disciples on those wonderfully memorable days in Galilee.

As we learn and value more about Jesus, he influences our moral decisions more deeply. He informs our conscience so that we become more capable of making good—life-giving—choices. And these choices will be the best they can be for our journey in God's love.

Conscience in action

> *Be open to the mind and heart and authority of Jesus.*

Can we misuse this teaching about the central role of conscience? Yes. We have described conscience as God's voice within us. But what if we are not aware of an interior place within? What if we are not aware that God dwells at the deep center of ourselves?

Some writers describe our society as one in which we are oriented to the world outside us, not to the inner life of our hearts and minds. This can mean that we take direction more from those around us than from our own inner voice. We consult the latest fashion magazines for what to wear; we voice opinions that reflect what we imagine others want us to say. To strengthen our conscience we can do any number of things:

(1) We can practice finding the still point within ourselves where God dwells; we can get in touch with ourselves, especially our deeper selves.

(2) We can use certain abiding moral principles to "test" whether our judgments are in line with God's ways. One of these principles is that the end never justifies an evil means. In other words, we may never do evil to bring about a good end. (Contrary to the legend of Robin Hood, stealing someone's coat to give to the poor is still wrong.)

(3) We can follow the golden rule: In everything, do unto others as you would have others do unto you. This simple principle contains great wisdom. To put the golden rule into practice requires a journey out of ourselves into another. That is, we must become empathetic or sensitive to the feelings and thoughts of others; we must stand in their shoes; we must look out at the world through their eyes. This kind of reaching out is itself a movement toward the good, a movement away from what might be disordered self-centeredness.

(4) We can open ourselves to the views of other good people and be respectful of these views. An overly tight grip on our own judgments can be a sign of a faulty conscience. An effective conscience is open to new learning. For Christians this openness includes, first of all, being open to the mind and heart and authority of Jesus. But for Catholics, the openness also includes the teaching voice of the church as it applies the mind and heart of Jesus to our times and circumstances.

The teaching role of the church is a gift from God. The teachings of the church are easily available to us; they are part of our collective wisdom—a wisdom that we can trace back to Jesus himself.

Some final thoughts on conscience

God is present within us.

The contemporary pluralistic world inundates us with many opinions or perspectives on what's going on. If one believes that the primary voice for determining good and evil, right from wrong, comes from outside us, then the image of moral chaos may seem appropriate. But if we know about the role of personal conscience and if we inform our conscious in a responsible way, then the present world of pluralism ceases to be a threat.

Rather, the world becomes an interesting social context for making choices. Why? Because we must consult our conscience if we are to make any sense out of this bewildering spectrum of moral opinion. In this moral chaos we become more aware of God's wisdom in providing us with an interior guide we call conscience. And always we can be sure—no matter what the TV or the papers or the radio blares—that God is present within us. God is for us. And if we listen to the voice of God gently and kindly speaking within us, we will know how and what to choose.

"I did the very best I knew how to do."

Most of us who are parents work hard, very hard. Day in and day out we strive to provide for our kids, to make sure they're safe, to help them learn and grow, and to encourage them to become good persons. And sometimes we goof up! At least that's what we tell ourselves, and we can get into a whole lot of parental self-blame if one of our own doesn't quite make the grade, so to speak. Why? Because we feel that we've failed.

Helping to form a child's conscience is a twenty-four-hour job. It's hard to know how we're doing in the middle of the journey. And other factors enter into how we raise our children: the community in which we live, the schools our children attend, the TV programs our children watch, the other families in our building or neighborhood, the presence or lack of role-modeling by other adults in our family.

In other words, a whole village—a global village—raises our child. We are all in this together. We bear responsibility for the world's children.

As parents who may think we goofed (whether we did or not), we must try to let go of the blame for our child's behavior. If he or she is now grown and responsible for his or her own actions and the consequences of these actions, we know in our hearts what we went through in raising this child. And whether or not that child "turned out" is something we can't do anything about now. We can't do anything now! Our influence is past history. Gone!

But we can do something about ourselves. We can tell ourselves something very important: "I did the very best I knew how to do. And if there was something I did or didn't do that I should have, I didn't know it then, I know it now.

A Psalm

The voice of the Lord is heard on the seas;
    the glorious God thunders,
    and God's voice echoes over the ocean.
The voice of the Lord is heard in all its might and majesty.
The voice of the Lord breaks the cedars . . .
The voice of the Lord makes the mountains of Lebanon
    jump like calves. . . .
    the lightning flash . . .
    the desert . . . shake. . . .
The Lord's voice shakes the oaks
    and strips the leaves from trees. . . .
The Lord gives strength to God's people
    and blesses them with peace.

From Psalm 29:3, 6–11

Bless Us with Peace

eace is a word we use often, dear God,
In this day and age.
As it applies to war and killing.

But know that we need some plain old peace in
    our lives too.
Sometimes our home is upside down with bedlam,
Sort of like a mild earthquake or hurricane.

Sometimes there's even war between those of us
Who live here in this house
As we hurt one another with words or deeds.
And sometimes we even have war within ourselves

About something we're thinking of doing,
Or have done already.

And it is in these times especially
That we need your help;
We need your advice;
We need to hear your voice,
We need your peace.

Amen.

CHAPTER FIVE

God's New Law Written in Our Hearts

A sister and a brother build up the kingdom of God's love . . .

The courthouse was like a beehive buzzing with the activity of many busy people. She sat on a hard bench just inside the door, waiting for her attorney. Her heart was sick; her body ached with lack of sleep and food. Confusion muddled her mind, and feelings wracked her body. Fear gripped her as she thought about seeing him in court. She had never imagined that this would happen to them.

"Oh, God, please help me." she prayed, "I'm so tired of it all. It isn't fair. I just want to die."

Then she heard someone call her name and looked up to see her only brother. Emotions overwhelmed her as she realized he was really standing there. An awkward quick hug and a swift kiss became signs of the depth of their feelings for one another.

"I didn't think I'd make it in time," he said. "The traffic was awful. How are you? Where's your lawyer?"

"I'm okay. She'll be here in a minute. Thanks for being here, Joey. I really never thought I'd need anybody here. But . . . oh, I'm so glad you came!" she added.

"There are some things a person shouldn't have to do alone. One is die, another is get divorced. Besides, we've got a lot of memories together; it'd be a shame to miss having this one too!" he quipped to break the seriousness of the moment.

As they sat down she found herself pouring her heart out to him. How she hadn't slept; how she couldn't eat; how the kids were hurting; how she was so scared to see Jeff.

Her brother just sat and listened. When she seemed to be finished, he gently took her hand and said, "Donna, no matter what happens today, no matter what happens tomorrow, there is one truth that none of us can ever erase. You and Jeff loved each other. And you loved those kids into this world. And never, ever will that reality change."

He gazed into her eyes and she saw both his love for her shining through and the truth of his message. As she nodded her head in realization, he continued.

"Love, as you felt it, was real. It was real for Jeff too. Who knows for sure how all this happened; how you both got to this day!"

She nodded. Her own thoughts about the past were muddled and confused. Hearing her brother's thoughts brought peace and an affirmation of that life she'd lived with Jeff. She looked at her brother intently, waiting for him to go on.

"Now, when the relationship is over, you're really finding a new beginning. Because tomorrow is coming and the next day and the next day. Soon, a year, then two, will be gone, and you will be more and more healed. And someday, because you've known love, you will feel it again. I know that in my heart, because I know you."

She looked at her little brother and cupped her other hand over his as it held hers. "Joey," she said, "I believe that, too, but I didn't think anyone else did. Oh, God, I'm so glad you came."

"My children, I shall not be with you very much longer. You will look for me; but I tell you now what I told the Jewish authorities, 'You cannot go where I am going.' And now I give you a new commandment: love one another. As I have loved you, so you must love one another. If you have love for one another, then everyone will know that you are my disciples."

John 13:33–35

Jesus tells us that love is a sign of the kingdom . . .

Jesus gathers with his friends. He knows his death is to come very soon; they do not. And during the course of doing almost a grand review of all he came to teach them, he goes a step further. He gives them a new commandment. Not one of the ten from the Hebrew Testament. But a new one that represents the new era that began with his coming to dwell amongst us. And this new invitation encompasses all he taught. The invitation is simple: Love one another. "That's all folks," he says. Simple. Yes. Yet, as we all know, challenging.

Jesus tells us something else here too. He tells us that others will recognize us as one of his followers when they see us love. How we act will show who and whose we are.

Some of our families meet terrible tragedies that have the potential to rip us apart. Let's think about those tragedies and how most of us respond. We strive to go on, to heal, to ask forgiveness, to give forgiveness as we try to act out of love—the way Jesus invites us to do. Then, comes healthy growth and healing.

No, everything does not suddenly come up roses and moonbeams, not by a long shot. But our family unit is still intact. The graces of the domestic church—the church of our home—are still there. When we serve and love one another, Jesus is with us, among us, in our home. We remain his disciples.

The woman and her brother in our opening story have an experience of giving and receiving love. God's new law is written in their hearts. The occasion is painful—a divorce hearing. Yet, their love for each other and the awareness of the reality of the love she and her husband once shared is very much a living out of Jesus' call to love one another. Her love continues. No matter what. And someday she will probably set that unreturned love gently aside and go on with her life.

In fact, with Jesus at her side, this is pretty much guaranteed.

"The entire Law of the Gospel is contained in the 'new commandment' *of Jesus, to love one another as he has loved us."*

CCC, 1970

God invites us to embrace the law of love.

Jesus was the greatest lawmaker of all time. We've probably never thought much about that truth because we have always considered the Hebrew Testament as the part of the Bible filled with laws. But many of us have felt that the Christian Testament contained few, if any, laws. That's really not true.

However, our confusion comes from the writings of Saint Paul. He preached that God's grace, not the Hebrew Law, saves us. Of course, he was creating a contrast between our salvation coming directly from God (in this view we are saved because God offers us life) and our salvation coming on the basis of our own efforts (here we are saved because we follow a set of laws). Paul emphasized God's great love for us—a love that is powerful and personal. Saint Paul put the spotlight on God's great love, not our efforts.

Toward the end of the time before Jesus' birth, Jeremiah, one of the last of the great prophets, wrote a curious statement about the Law. He was writing about the restoration of the Hebrew people after two devastating exiles: one in which the Assyrians took the people into exile and another in which the Babylonians led them away from their homeland.

Jeremiah lived to see the invaders destroy Judah and the Temple. But the prophet did not lose hope in the God of his people, the God of the covenant. He saw the coming of a new day when God would "make a new covenant with the people of Judah." In Jeremiah's writings, God says that God will put the "law within them and write it on their hearts. I will be their God and they will be my people." (Jeremiah. 31:31 and 33)

The full meaning of this did not become clear until the coming of Jesus. Matthew's Gospel, written primarily for Jewish converts to Christianity, provides ample comparisons between the old and the new law. We find these comparisons toward the beginning of the gospel in what we call Jesus' Sermon on the Mount.

In his sermon, Jesus says that in the old law adultery is committing the act itself. However, in the new law, adultery is possible simply by desire. Murder in the old law was killing without proper cause; in the new law anger can be a form of murder. Perhaps the most radical statement Jesus makes on the mountain that day is this:

> "You have heard that it was said, 'Love your friends, hate your enemies.' But now I tell you: love your enemies and pray for those who persecute you, so that you may become children of your Father in heaven."
>
> *From Matthew 5:43–45*

Jesus spells out the new law as something done both in action and in thought. He stresses what Jeremiah pointed out. That God has written the new law not on the hard stone tablets of Sinai but on the soft tablets of our hearts.

Right and wrong in the kingdom of God is determined by what's within our heart. By the love in our heart. Jesus' teaching here may sound simpler than the teachings of the Hebrew Testament, but it's not. For Jesus is calling us to a conversion of heart.

How do we convert our heart? We turn to God, we stand in all truth and humility before God, and we live a life that reflects the goodness and holiness of our God. We act like God acts. That is the new law. Jesus summed up for us what this new law means when he said, "You must be perfect—just as your Father in heaven is perfect." (Matthew 5:48) Sound impossible? Too idealistic? Beyond human possibility? Exactly.

A new day with new expectations

The statements Jesus made sometimes threw his closest friends against the hard wall of their own beliefs. Statements like "if you are asked to walk a mile with someone, walk two" or "pray for your enemies" and so forth. With these statements, Jesus isn't really creating laws. Instead, he's describing a certain way—his way—of responding to life's situations.

Jesus came to invite us to be a part of a new arrangement between God and us. God was inviting us to participate in God's own life. God's own Spirit lives within us and with us and through us. We are, so to speak, walking sanctuaries.

Jesus begins his ministry with the simple declaration that the kingdom of God is at hand. It has begun. It is as if he's saying, "With my being here, the kingdom is here. Turn your hearts to God and repent. We're now operating on a new set of rules around here."

God is now giving us more; so God expects more from us. And what more does God give us? The example of Jesus and the grace of the Spirit. After the coming of the Holy Spirit at Pentecost, the apostles lost their fear and charged outside to tell everyone about Jesus. Just before that, they had pretended that they didn't even know Jesus. What's the lesson here? Without God, we can do little; with God, all is possible! No limits!

Many of us who are Christians remain unaware of the teaching of Scripture and the church about the transforming power of grace. Let's explore this a little: Jesus came to invite us to be a part of a new arrangement between God and us. God was inviting us to participate in God's own life.

When we embrace all that Jesus is, we connect more deeply with God. God's own Spirit lives within us and with us and through us. We are, so to speak, walking sanctuaries. God "graces" us. That means that just as we were created first in our mother's womb, so we are now re-created by the work of God. We are new beings, adopted into God's family.

The waters of Christian baptism symbolize new life. The actions of the sacrament make us members of the body of Christ Jesus. In fact, we *are* the body of Christ. None of this is accomplished through our own power or effect. All of it is God's work; work God delights in doing!

We are all children of God—dear, beloved, cherished little ones of God. We are all sisters and brothers. This was the most common way those early Christians referred to each other. They believed in this family relationship. They felt it. And their belief and the relationship itself made a big difference in how they related to each other.

All Christians are sisters and brothers of each other: Catholics, Episcopalians, Baptists, and all those who belong to all those little local churches scattered everywhere. We're all family members. We all have the same parent—God. Perhaps ninety-nine percent of what makes us *us* is the same in God's eyes, and one percent (that may be a bit high) is different.

The obvious question is this: Do we appear to act as if we believe this? Do we extend our love and compassion and generosity and kindness and understanding and welcome to all Christians? All?

And what about those other human beings who do not profess an explicit relationship to Jesus? Many of them, of course, never even heard of Jesus. Yet they are our sisters and brothers too.

Again, a brief review of the basics of our faith may help us out here. First, there is only one God. Different people may use different names for God, but there is only one God. Further, different people will understand God differently, but God remains the same; we all just think differently about God. We Christians believe that Jesus is the savior of all—whether people know this or not. The savior of *all!* There is not one kind of redeeming grace for Christians and another kind for everyone else.

Thus, we Christians believe that when we come to our eternity with God—in God's love, which is heaven—the only difference between Christians and other people will be that Christians may be less surprised at who's already there than the other people will. Why? Because we believe in the inclusivity of our God. God loves us all—Christian and non-Christian. God gathers all of us into God's deep and abiding love. Between all of us, God wants there to exist a sure solidarity.

Accepting the person of Jesus brings a change in us. The Spirit of Jesus empowers us in ways we can hardly imagine. Our life is still firmly rooted in our humanity, but we are transformed. The new law does not so much tell us what to do. Instead, it tells us to be who we are—children of God, followers of Jesus, wellsprings of the Spirit.

Sanctity and ordinary Christians

Some historians say that the Roman emperors martyred the early Christians because of their view of human relations and society. Roman society was layered. Rome assigned everyone a position, a place in society. Roman society underscored these differences.

What bothered the authorities so much was that the Christians welcomed everyone who wanted to join in. Slaves and free people, Greeks and Jews, and even women and children!

Then along came this movement called Christianity. We Christians gathered to be together, to pray together, and to break bread together. And what bothered the authorities so much was that the Christians welcomed everyone who wanted to join in. Slaves and free people, Greeks and Jews, and even women and children!

And these Christians accepted each other as equals—sisters and brothers. The Romans knew that if the movement spread throughout the Empire, the glory days were over. What would the leaders do without their privileges of status or of rank and without the power over others that went with it?

Saint Paul describes the various roles that are ours as we follow Jesus. God gives the roles; God graces the role-taker; God sees all as equally important. All of us are equal before God.

When Jesus' new law went from the outside to the inside of us, it eliminated powerful positions in society. The new law negated three kinds of differences. People had different roles, yes, but these were only different, not unequal. In his many writings, Saint Paul describes the various roles that are ours as we follow Jesus. God gives the roles; God graces the role-taker; God sees all as equally important; God plays no favorites. Each of us is a favorite of God. All of us are equal before God.

Throughout its history, the Catholic Church has named certain people as saints. In other words, the church has said that these people—women and men—have exhibited heroic virtue; they have lived in accord with their understanding of what God asked of them. The first saints the church canonized (gave the title of saint) were those whom the Romans martyred.

The saints—all of them—are a wonderful mix of folks. Some told jokes while being cooked in oil for their faith. A few rose to the ceiling when they prayed.

One tried to walk on water and was successful until he noticed what he was doing, then he sank. One, when tempted by an impure thought, threw himself into a thorn bush. And some just prayed and thought and wrote wonderful books about their faith.

In many, many different ways these saints loved God and their neighbor. And because the church likes to offer us examples of living the Christian life, it canonized these people and said that they now live on for all eternity in God's love.

But are there many saints or only a few? Only a few, if we talk about canonized saints; many, many more if we talk about ordinary ones. Who are these "ordinary" saints? They are those of us who truly live as children of God. Those of us who love God and our neighbor in simple, ordinary ways. Those of us who live in accordance with the new law of love etched on our hearts.

God invites all of us to be saints, and all of us, with God's help, can be. The challenges and the comforts of the Christian life are for all of us.

Most of us are rather ordinary folk. We're many colors and sizes. We may be students or retired folks; we may be married or single. Some of us are divorced; some, widows or widowers. Some of us are children; some, grandparents. Some of us have jobs and some are unemployed. Some of us are rich; some, poor; but most of us are in-between these two conditions. Some are straight and some are gay. We are all somewhat different, but we also have a great deal in common. Unfortunately, we often focus on our differences and forget what we share—what we have in common.

God invites all of us to be saints, and all of us, with God's help, can be. The challenges and the comforts of the Christian life are for all of us. The new law knows no boundaries. It's as wide as the boundless love of God from which it comes. We can live the Christian life (we can be saints) because God helps us to do so. Our God is a generous God. The love of God is abundant, and God's generosity reaches to the corners of the universe. It reaches into each nook and cranny of our hearts.

"The charity of Christ is the source in us of all our merits *before God. Grace, by uniting us to Christ in active love, ensures the supernatural quality of our acts and consequently their merit before God and before men. The saints have always had a lively awareness that their merits were pure grace.*"

CCC, 2011

In our family we grow into the love of God.

The Catholic Church has taught for only a short time that other Christian people besides we Catholics are part of the church. The teaching began in the early sixties when the series of meetings called Vatican II happened. And for many of us, these new teachings brought a flood of questions: Can the teachings of the church really change? Can we grow in our understanding of our faith? If our beliefs change, are we still Catholics?

Let's remember that change is part of being human and that the church is a living entity—the body of Christ. We are a people who change and grow. Thus, we are a church that changes and grows.

And this is both a blessing and a difficulty. Why? Because we don't all agree; we don't all understand the same thing at the same time in the same way. God's revelation comes gently into our being. And sometimes determining if the revelation is from God or from ourselves is difficult. As church, we know success and failure, struggle and joy.

We are not, and have never been, perfect. All of us (from the millions of believers and leaders in the past to the present ones) are capable of mistakes and misunderstandings about Jesus' teachings. And in spite of the fact that Jesus is the core of our faith, we sometimes forget what the core teaching of our church is—Christ Jesus. We preach a person, not a dogma.

We must go back—again and again—to the Scriptures and see what Jesus said and did. When we do this, new insights come to us, new understandings of old insights. Then, because we have a clearer understanding of who Jesus is for us and what he revealed and proclaimed, we must sometimes change what we teach. This is good, and this happens because we are a living church of people.

This is true in family too. We don't know all of those who came before us. We look at old photos and see (for the most part) unsmiling black and white images staring at us with worn faces and weary eyes and starched clothes.

Someday our future family members will look at us and think and feel some of the same things we feel when we look at the photos of the past! We don't see our ancestors in "living color," so to speak. We see them as flat, nonreal persons who don't mean much to us. And that may be how future generations will look at us.

But all this changes when we study our roots, our family of origin. We discover that we have inherited Great-Grandpa Rudy's nose, that we cut our ham like Aunt Gracie, that a long genetic history of alcoholism haunts our family. We discover, sometimes to our dismay, that all those who came on this earth before us (all the way back to Jesus and beyond) have influenced us.

There's a wonderful way of diagramming our family history by doing what's called a genogram. This is a picture of our lineage with little boxes and circles. The difference between this and a regular family tree is that it welcomes nicknames, shows relationships, delineates the passing down of names and the presence of genetic behavior (such as alcoholism) and learned behavior (such as abuse) in our family. With a genogram, we can even trace the traditions that enrich the way we celebrate Christmas.

Discovering and uncovering those unique people before us is an opportunity to know both ourselves and our God better. One of the greatest things we can discover is how our ancestors loved one another in family and how we love one another. Just like the brother and sister in the opening story. Was that court-house experience holy? Yes! Loving and caring about each other is doing what Jesus intended. This kind of activity shows the life of the domestic church in a simple yet profound way.

In our family tree we find saints and sinners. Actually, we find sanctity in sinners for all of us are both at various times in our lives. Doing the genogram helps us see this. Tracing our family ties can be both fun and insightful. Doing this can be a gift we give to ourselves and to those who will someday look at pictures (or videos) of us!

"'All Christians in any state or walk of life are called to the fullness of Christian life and to the perfection of charity.' All are called to holiness: 'Be perfect, as your heavenly Father is perfect.'"

In order to reach this perfection the faithful should use the strength dealt out to them by Christ's gift, so that . . . doing the will of the Father in everything, they may wholeheartedly devote themselves to the glory of God and to the service of their neighbor. Thus the holiness of the People of God will grow in fruitful abundance, as is clearly shown in the history of the Church through the lives of so many saints. (Lumen Gentium 40§2)

CCC, 2013

A Psalm

The storm makes my heart beat wildly. / Listen, all of you, to the voice of God, / to the thunder that comes from his mouth. / He sends the lightning across the sky, / from one end of the earth to the other. / Then the roar of his voice is heard, / the majestic sound of thunder, / and all the while the lightning flashes. / At God's command amazing things happen, / wonderful things that we can't understand. . . . / He brings our work to a stop; / he shows us what he can do.

Psalm 37:1–5, 7–8

I Don't Want to Dry Up

Loving one another, dear God, certainly is
the hardest thing to do!
Sure, it's easy when we're holding
a cuddly little baby
Or eating fresh chocolate chip cookies
Made with love by someone else.
But, O God, it's not so easy in the middle of the night
When that same baby won't go to sleep.

And loving each other isn't always easy either
When the chocolate chip cookies seem to be
A bribe to mow the lawn
Or do some other yucky job.

And loving each other isn't easy either,
When someone won't change
And so I'm the one who has to change and put up
with it!

But it's sure a good thing you stayed around
To help love be real!

So now all we need is for you to keep on helpin'
And we'll keep on workin' at it!

Amen.

CHAPTER SIX

Loving Both Neighbors and Strangers

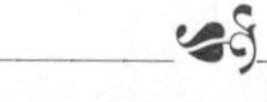

A son returns home, longing for love . . .

"Will you get that please?" the harried woman yelled. "If it's for your father, he's in the garage!"

"Hello? Yup. Just a second," the sixteen-year-old said and then hollered, "It's for you or Dad!"

Her mother turned off the vacuum and headed for the phone. "Boy, I'll never get the Saturday list done this way!" she thought.

"Hello, this is Jeanne. . . . Who? . . . I'm sorry, I don't know your name. Oh . . . yes, Brian has mentioned you, come to think of it. Now I remember. You two met last year. Are you in town? I mean . . . what can I do for you?"

The young man at the other end was speaking slowly, softly. But she heard him anyway. Brian was sick. And his friend was bringing him home, tonight. In fact, they were on the road.

"Let me talk to Brian," the worried mother demanded, confused and scared as to why her twenty-two-year-old wasn't calling himself.

"I'm sorry. Brian didn't want me to call. He just wanted to come. We're at a rest stop, and he's coming, so I have to go. I just wanted to warn you. Good-bye," he said and hung up.

She stood there in disbelief, as if the phone conversation hadn't happened. Fear started to inch its way up her back and to weaken her knees. "What on earth?" she thought and went to get her husband.

Brian and his friend didn't get home for hours. As the minutes slowly crept by, the parents imagined all sorts of terrible possibilities. Including, of course, AIDS. But then, they quickly discounted that. Brian couldn't have AIDS! It just wasn't possible.

When they finally heard the sound of the car pulling up in the driveway, both parents jumped up and ran for the door to their son. "Brian!" his mother yelled across the yard. "What a surprise! Oh, and you brought a friend!" she faked.

"He looks fine," she said quietly to her husband. In fact, Brian looked better than when he'd been home at Christmas.

"Hi, Mom, Hi, Dad!" he said and hugged his mother. "This is Karl, from school. Remember?"

It was then she heard his wheezing. He seemed to be trying to get enough breath to speak. "Brian, what's the matter?" she asked. "You sound sick."

"I have a lung problem, Mom. And the doctor thought I should come home for a while. So Karl brought me."

Silently she thanked God for Karl being there to bring him home. "We can deal with that! You know how good ol' mom can make you feel better! Boy, I was afraid you had something terrible like AIDS," she quipped.

"I do, Mom." her child said.

But the teacher of the Law wanted to justify himself, so he asked Jesus, "Who is my neighbor?"

Jesus answered, "There was once a man who was going down from Jerusalem to Jericho when robbers attacked him, stripped him, and beat him up, leaving him half dead. It so happened that a priest was going down that road; but when he saw the man, he walked on by on the other side. In the same way a Levite also came there, went over and looked at the man, and then walked on by on the other side. But a Samaritan who was traveling that way came upon the man, and when he saw him, his heart was filled with pity. He went over to him, poured oil and wine on his wounds and bandaged them; then he put the man on his own animal and took him to an inn, where he took care of him. The next day he took out two silver coins and gave them to the innkeeper. 'Take care of him,' he told the innkeeper, 'and when I come back this way, I will pay you whatever else you spend on him.' "

And Jesus concluded, "In your opinion, which one of these three acted like a neighbor toward the man attacked by the robbers?"

The teacher of the Law answer, "The one who was kind to him."

Jesus replied, "You go, then, and do the same."

Luke 10:29–37

A man lies by the side of the room needing love . . .

This scriptural story is a great example of neighborlove. Neighbor is anyone, related or not, near or far, known or unknown. Anyone; everyone.

The parents in our opening story have come upon their own son along the road of life; he's stricken with AIDS. And now the hard part. Will they be the priest who ambled on by? The Levite (who might work in the

Temple) who stared and then turned away? Or the Samaritan (a member of a break-away church) who loved the man back to health?

Thousands of friends, families, and neighbors face this dilemma. The young man and his friend in our opening story could be gay, we're not told. Unfortunately, most of us probably wondered, and this is what happens in our real life—we assume things about persons who are diagnosed as HIV-positive or as having AIDS. In the poignant story from the New Testament, Jesus teaches us that who the person is or what the person does or did must not matter to us. What must matter very much, however, is that he or she needs help.

Some of us choose to help a person living with AIDS only after we know if the person had the unfortunate experience of acquiring the disease in some "acceptable way." What's "acceptable?" Having hemophilia; living with a marital partner who has gone astray; being born to a mother who's HIV-positive. Others of us simply help, no matter what or when or why or where or how.

The family in our story has great pain to go through. The coming days and weeks and months won't be easy. We hope they love their son through his death as much as they loved him through his life. And we pray for their courage and generosity to do so.

Being HIV-positive and living with AIDS are problems of the whole human family. We all have AIDS. That is, the disease belongs to the human family. It is both our reality and our responsibility. The Samaritan in our story acted because of the need he saw and recognized. Which of us are good Samaritans today?

Jesus asks us to love one another as he has first loved us.

We can summarize the new law in the words Jesus used at the Last Supper: "As I have loved you, so you must love one another." (John 13:34) Those who first heard him say this probably winced a bit because they knew from personal experience what he was really saying. They knew just how much and how far Jesus loved.

At that supper on the day before he died, Jesus gave his apostles just what they didn't want to hear: A commandment calling for love at a depth hardly imaginable. They had seen his love in action; they knew his love because they had walked and talked and eaten and prayed with him. They had seen how he loved each of them.

Once Jesus told them to love as he had loved them, they each probably took a deep breath and thought, "Do we really want to go through with this?" Coming up with a ready response to his invitation wasn't easy. Perhaps Peter mulled over the new commandment for long, agonizing moments and out of his confusion came his denial of Jesus a few hours later.

This was no pie-in-the-sky movement the apostles had joined. This was serious business! They might have preferred almost anything to that new commandment! They might have later on asked the apostle John, who seemed to remember these kinds of things, to repeat again exactly what Jesus had said. But they had heard correctly; he *had* said, "As I have loved you, so you must love one another." Days after that last supper, when they thought about his words, their throats became dry. For by this time, they had lived through his crucifixion.

What kind of love is this?

The marketplace feeds us thousands of images of love.

When we hear the new commandment to love our neighbor, we are at a distinct disadvantage. The word *love* can confuse us. Why? Because the word *love* is terribly overused in our society; in fact, it may be the most misunderstood word in our entire vocabulary. Having learned that people are starved for love, the mass media—Hollywood, Madison Avenue, and the tabloids—have raced to give us their version of what they think we crave. Thus, the confusion.

The marketplace has begun to exploit love. Whatever is sold on the movie screens and in magazines often has to have a love dimension. Some of it is like thick maple syrup; some is as clean as the windows in a showroom of new cars; some is as painful and tragic as a plane crash. The marketplace feeds us, and continues to feed us, thousands of images and portraits of love.

Let's try to bring some clarity to our Christian understanding of love. Let's try to find how we can remain faithful to Jesus' message. We really don't have a choice about doing this because Jesus has told us that if we are his followers we will love. He said that love of neighbor would be the great sign to others about who were the real Christians. Pretty cut and dried! Pretty hard!

As we attempt to love, we must look first to the person and the life of Jesus himself. How did he love? For starters, he seemed to love everyone! Those who seemed open to his love; those who tried to destroy him and his message of God's love for everyone; and those who tried to discredit his teachings, put down his background, or just embarrass him in public. Still he loved all of them, in spite of the fact that most of the people who knew about him didn't love him back.

In all situations, Jesus simply moved about searching for opportunities to love. And he expressed his love both by befriending others and by responding to their needs if that was a good thing to do. His love was thoughtful and specific, never sentimental. Jesus would encounter a person, establish a relationship, and then ask what he could do to help that person become better.

Jesus expressed his love in action. He used whatever he possessed—his presence, his time, his energy, and his connection to God—to help others.

Sometimes the people who encountered him needed only to talk—like Nicodemus who secretly visited him one night. Other people needed more wine at a wedding feast when the marketplace was closed. Some people asked to be cured—physically, mentally, spiritually. In every meeting, with every person, Jesus did what he could, given the circumstances. (Of course, Jesus did not always do what people asked of him because he knew the request was not in the best interests of the one asking.)

We also know that Jesus spoke about the fullest possible expression of neighborlove—the giving of one's life for others. He did this action too; he died on the cross for us. And that act above all has been the most powerful expression of Christian love down through the centuries.

But martyrdom does not always mean a final death, a giving of our life one time. Rather, martyrdom today means a day-by-day event in which we give love to others with generosity and sensitivity—and we not use a calculator to estimate the cost of our giving.

The mass media seldom tell us about this kind of love. But daily, hourly, we love this way. And we do not seek applause or approval or fame or fortune for the love we give so unstintingly. No, we love for the sake of the person who calls forth our love. Just as Jesus did.

Let's return to the story of the good Samaritan. Jesus sets the story on the road from Jerusalem to Jericho. It was a dangerous road then as it is today. Someone robs and beats and leaves a man for dead on that road.

And what happens? First a priest sees the man in obvious need and passes by. He even moves to the other side of the road to give the impression that he doesn't see the traveler in need. But who is he kidding?

Then a Levite, the family from which priests came, passed by. Same response.

Finally, a Samaritan passes by. He's outside his territory, for Samaria lies to the north. Someone could waylay, attack, and even kill him on that road for the people of Judea do not like the Samaritans. From the standpoint of Jews at that time, Samaritans were traitors who had left the faith and worshiped in Samaria instead of at the Temple in Jerusalem.

Thus, we see the tension, the high drama, in this story. The Samaritan should not be near Jerusalem and should not be on this dangerous road. If anyone had an excuse to pass by, it was this man! But did he ignore the traveler who lay cut and bleeding on the road? No. He stopped, which was risky in itself, and cared for the battered man. He soothed his wounds. Then he lifted him atop his donkey and took him to an inn—a hotel of the times.

That night the sick man was probably in a coma, needing care. And the good Samaritan gave it to him. The next morning, the Samaritan had to leave, but not before giving the innkeeper enough money to take care of his newfound friend. In fact, he promised to pay whatever was due the care when he returned that way.

The fact that the good Samaritan promised to take care of the "tab" tells us what true neighborlove is about. When we meet the need of a neighbor, we must use our heart and our head and not count the cost!

Let's put Jesus' story in a more contemporary setting. Two modern parents on this road of life come across one of their own attacked by the terrible AIDS virus. And there is nothing their son, Brian, can do—except seek help. He is off to the side of road, so to speak, and terribly in need. A cure is not possible. He needs the care of those who love him. And we all hope—and pray—that his family gives him this care. We know the truth: God often invites parents to be good Samaritans—especially to their own children.

Basic love of neighbor

The word most often used for love in the New Testament is the Greek word *agape*. We might translate it as altruistic or generous love. It is loving that involves giving. The focus in agape love is on the other, on the one in need. And we can think of need in very basic terms: We often have a need for the simple presence of another person. Just being with someone can be very loving. In fact, it is often very, very loving.

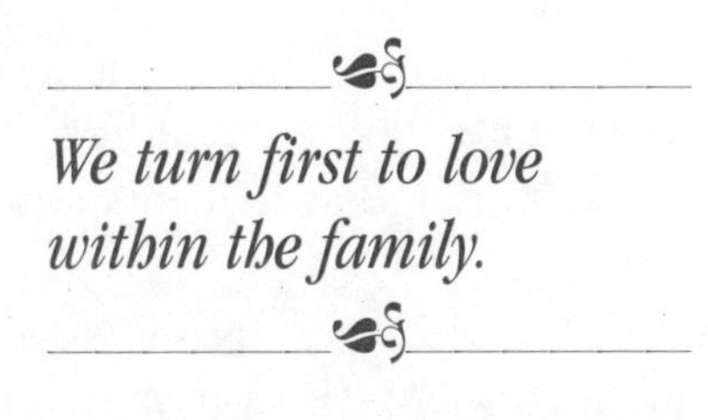

In our familystyle catechism, we rightfully turn first to love within the family itself. And this is often a very challenging kind of love. When we live with someone long enough, we have the privilege of knowing all his or her good and not-so-good qualities. So we might think of the neighborlove of our family members as most important. This would especially be true of married families in which the spouses are "neighborly" to one another!

When we talk of our "neighborloving" family, we're clearly talking about very close neighbors! We need to apply the Gospel to the immediate settings of our life. (Imagining heroic love in some distant place while ignoring the needs of those with whom we now live can be a terrible hypocrisy!)

The Ten Commandments deal with love of God and love of neighbor. The first commandment that deals with social life (relating to other human beings) is that of honoring our mother and our father. Most Catholics learned about this commandment while still quite young. By far the biggest relationship in our life was to our parent or caregiver. In the New Testament, we also found other texts that called for children to obey their parents, so we concluded that this commandment applied to children.

By far the biggest relationship in our life was to our parent.

What's interesting, however, is that this commandment (the Fourth Commandment) is not about children obeying their parents, but rather about adults honoring their own parents! In the more primitive culture of the biblical Jews, children were easily kept in tow. Parents were bigger and they had control! So from the standpoint of maintaining the society, the Jews didn't need a special commandment for children and their parents.

Since that is so, why do we have the Fourth Commandment? Because in biblical times many of the elderly could no longer take care of themselves. To survive, they needed their grown children to care for them. They had a great need for protection, for care, and for love. Thus, the Fourth Commandment dealt with this very important issue. Yes, the commandment *did* apply to family, but to a different family relationship than parent and young child. Probably a surprise for most of us!

The rest of the commandments have a similar family application. Commandment Five (Don't kill) tells us that life is the most precious resource of a family. If we're married, we don't commit adultery (Commandment Six) for that action can weaken or even devastate our family. Commandment Seven asks us not to steal from another household, another family, because its members need what they possess to survive.

Commandment Eight asks us to tell the truth because making false statements about others, especially family members, also weakens relationships that need trust and honesty to remain strong. In fact, we mustn't even think about and desire what belongs to another family (Commandments Nine and Ten). Why? Because coveting (lusting after someone or something) could lead to actions that hurt that family and our own.

All these commandments are familytalk; they are rules to help our families survive and even thrive. Biblical morality begins with family life. It doesn't end there, of course, but if it doesn't start there, it will fail to be real anywhere else. This is a truth we need to learn over and over again.

Jesus tells us to love our neighbor. Not a don't, but a do!

The Old Testament states most of the Ten Commandments negatively. That is, don't do this; don't do that. In the New Testament, however, the new commandment is more positive. Jesus tells us to love our neighbor. Not a don't, but a do! Jesus encourages us to do good to those who persecute us; to pray for our enemies; to offer hospitality to the stranger.

In his small book *On the Family,* Pope John Paul II says,

> The family, which is founded and given life by love, is a community of persons: . . . Its first task is to live with fidelity the reality of communion in a constant effort to develop an authentic community of persons. The inner principle of that task, its permanent power and its final goal, is love: Without love the family is not a community of persons and in the same way, without love the family cannot live, grow and perfect itself as a community of persons. (18)

The word *persons* here contains a rich human meaning. Acknowledging that each family member is a real person is a relatively recent idea. Most of us today have no difficulty in accepting that women and children are equal to men, that we are all persons. However, that truth was not so clear and obvious as recently as one hundred years ago. In some parts of the world this basic idea has yet to take root.

Added to the affirmation of personhood is the call for love throughout our family. Love is at the heart of family life. Our family is the first school of love (a phrase used by the pope). And all the members of our family are enrolled in that school.

Neighborlove begins at home and moves outward. That is God's wisdom and God's plan. Sadly, love does not always work that way. Sometimes family members inflict deep and tragic pain on one another. But that is part of the real world too. Sin and sainthood are both very real. If love is to be true, however, it must begin at home.

We learn to love in families and then we reach across to our neighbors—near and far.

Our best and worst critics are the members of our own family. Acceptance by family (which we translate to being loved or not) is at the heart of our feeling good about ourselves as human beings, as children of God. If our love-relationships within our family are not positive, nurturing, and encouraging, we find that loving others is hard.

Without the experience of being loved and of loving within family, we find it harder to know how to love. The ongoing family experience is so important if we are to become loving people. *Ongoing* is an extremely important word here. Family is an ongoing event; we are always susceptible to being loved or hurt by our family members.

Our formation time in family (those years of learning how to be good, loving, and responsible human beings) is key. However, the following years of living out that formation are also very important to us. We can never undo being family. We may try, but we can't leave behind what is bred into the marrow of our bones.

Jesus used family language all the time. He said that if we are about to offer our gift at the altar and remember our brother (by which he meant sister, mother, father, child, neighbor, relative, friend, stranger) has something against us, we must leave the altar and make up with our brother. This wasn't by accident. Jesus thought in terms of family relationships. He even used the word *family* to include those who followed him.

The caring and concern between family members is holy; it is an ordinary expression of Jesus' love. Familylove is the primary kind of neighborlove.

Neighborlove is a wonderful word we've coined in this familystyle catechism to talk about the invitation Jesus gives us to join him in living our love for other human beings. *Familylove* is the first type of neighborlove, and it is the most important because with familylove we first live our Christian life of following Jesus.

If we think about what happened today in the world of our family, would we be able to identify the holy loving that happened within our household? Did someone make a dinner? Do the wash? Call a relative? Help with homework? Change a tire? Plant a garden? Find the dog? Sit and laugh? Cry with one of us?

In these and thousands of other ways, we love just as Jesus invited us to love. As we lovingly serve our family, goodness and holiness grow in our midst. And then we reach out to our neighbors, to our global community, and share with them the Spirit of love.

Since the biblical time of the tower of Babel—a time that pride caused humanity to break into diverse and warring factions—we have seen the "problems" brought about by religious differences.

Many wars, even those of our own era, have at their roots religious roots. Have you ever wondered what God thinks about when people kill each other motivated by their assumed relationship with God? Is there not something against logic and reason in this situation? Are not we all children of the *same* God?

Of course, when we look at "the big picture," the stupidity and the tragedy of the so-called "wars of religion" make little sense. Useless killing for an unfounded reason.

But it happens and far too often. We are still learning what it means to be a neighbor in God's neighborhood!

And perhaps, saddest of all is when religious differences pull family members apart from each other.

Our faith is built on love and respect much more than on hostility and destructive judgments.

Jesus once said that it is fairly easy to love one's friends. After all, we agree with each other on most everything. Anybody can do that. But Jesus added that if you wanted to think and act as he does, then one is challenged to love not only friends, but enemies—the ones who are different. The ones whom God loves as much as God loves us. Perhaps the riskiest of all acts of love. Do you need to do that? Consider how you might do it. God will be there too.

"The apostle St. Paul reminds us of this: 'He who loves his neighbor has fulfilled the law. The commandments, "You shall not commit adultery, You shall not kill, You shall not steal, You shall not covet," *and any other commandment, are summed up in this sentence, "You shall love your neighbor as yourself." Love does no wrong to a neighbor; therefore love is the fulfilling of the law.'"*

CCC, 2196

A Psalm

You know how I am insulted, / how I am disgraced and dishonored; / you see all my enemies. / Insults have broken my heart, / and I am in despair. / I had hoped for sympathy, but there was none; / for comfort, but I found none. / When I am hungry, they gave me poison; / when I was thirsty, they offered me vinegar.

Psalm 69:19–21

Being Neighborly

ost of us live close to somebody else—
In our apartment or house,
Across the hall, across the street,
or down the road a piece.

Neighbors, they call us.
Neighbors.
It has a good ring to it.
Makes one think of hometowns,
Of friends moved away,
Of childhood friends
And neighborhood fun.

Good stuff.

Neighbor stuff.
Yet, you said, Lord Jesus, that
Even those "others" are our neighbors.
Those across town
Or across the world—
Perhaps a different color
Or religion
Or family structure
Or ethnic group
Or sexual orientation
All of them, and more,
Are our neighbors too.

Some of us live as if our life is ours alone.
Others live life alone.
We all need to get together! Amen.

CHAPTER SEVEN

The Wondrous Gift of Life, Love, and Sexuality

A grandson is surprised by what his grandpa knows about love . . .

"Hi Grandpa. Where's Grandma?" the sixteen-year-old asked.

"She's at the store. She'll be right back," he answered.

The young man plopped down in a well-worn chair and moaned.

"Boy, it sounds like you really need to sit down. What's the matter?" his grandfather asked.

Not wanting to hurt the older man's feelings, the boy just said, "Oh, nothin', Grandpa."

"Well if a moan like that came out of me, it'd be a whole lot more than nothing!"

"Just girl problems, Grandpa. Something you probably wouldn't understand. It's a whole lot different now."

The old man looked at him with a smile that was part grin, part smirk. "Sounds like you're searching for answers to old questions."

"I'm not looking for answers! I just want to understand what girls want. They're so confusing. First they come on to you—I mean flirt, Grandpa—and then the next thing you know they're going the other way. I don't understand!"

He sighed again and looked at the ceiling as if looking for some help from above. When his grandfather said nothing, the boy took that as an invitation to continue and said, "Well, like today. There's this girl . . . she likes me, and I got the word out that I liked her."

"Yes."

"Well, so I go up to her and say 'Hi' and stuff. And what happens? She was real nice, but then when I asked her if she wanted a ride home, she freaked and said she had to go. She gives me this dumb grin and walks away. So I took off and came home. I give up! I don't get it!" the boy-becoming-man said.

His grandfather leaned back in his own chair and confided, "I'll bet she's shy. The 'dumb grin' as you call it, gives her away."

The boy looked at his grandfather with renewed interest. "Really?"

"Yes. Now the question is was there a light in her eyes? Did she sort of flip her head or her hair as she walked away? Did she do it looking slightly over her shoulder? Did she go away slowly with lots of movement, you know what I mean?"

The young man sat there with a dumb look of his own. He was, in fact, thunderstruck. How did Grandpa know what happened? He just sat there—bemused—looking at the grin on his grandfather's face and the gleam in his eye.

"A healthy tree does not bear bad fruit, not does a poor tree bear good fruit. Every tree is known by the fruit it bears; you do not pick figs from thorn bushes or gather grapes from bramble bushes. A good person brings good out of the treasure of good things in his heart; a bad person brings bad out of his treasure of bad things. For the mouth speaks what the heart is full of."

Luke 6:43-45

Jesus surprises us with his thoughts on bringing forth life . . .

This passage from the Gospel of Luke could very well be about parenting! And grandparenting! And any other caregiving of children and families! It could be about nurturing and guiding and educating and modeling and living good and wholesome lives. And about recognizing that the family is, in fact, the primary community; that from the heart of the family comes the child—the fruit. And, in a very wonderful ending line, this scriptural passage tells us that we speak (that is "live") that which we have learned.

What a great affirmation of the gifts of a family! But also, what a wonderful invitation to pay attention to the power we have to make or break the future generations—our children and our children's children. For a poor tree does not bear good fruit. That's why we must enter this experience called family with openness and a willingness to learn. None of us knows everything about how to parent, and so we make mistakes. But if we share our stories of life with one another, the fruit (our children) can recognize life's learning in our lives.

The grandfather in our opening story is doing just that. His grandson is shocked that his Grandpa (no less!) knows anything about girls! What a wonderful memory for the two of them! Although the world was probably very different when the older man was younger, some things never change. And the God-given attraction of male and female is a wonderful gift our God has given us.

Families are indeed like living trees, going through season after season, always changing and becoming more. And the gift of sexuality—the image of God in two persons, male and female—is both a mystery discovered and a mystery still unfolding. When the Scriptures mention the image of God, they refer to our being created male and female. Thus, we express ourselves as the image of God particularly through the two genders. Sexual duality (twoness) reveals God.

Today we witness more fathers in a nurturing role and more mothers in various leadership roles outside the family. We are learning about God's great wisdom in creating us male and female, and God looked at what had been done and said, then and now, "It's good; very good."

Another thing we're learning about sexual duality is that we are created to be interdependent, to share a healthy dependence and independence at the same time. God intended us to be equals. Yes, we are different, but our differences work sideways, not up and down. That is to say, we are equals, peers, partners.

We must try to create a culture that welcomes and accepts equality. We caregivers of children can help this reality come to be. And perhaps future generations will tell stories of how women—a part of the image of God—were once (in the old days!) considered less than men—the other part of the image of God. And in those future days, people will marvel at the way we changed this perception. The future will accept all of us simply as persons made in the image and likeness of God.

In the meantime, we can all go about our challenging work of helping our families and others understand the wonderful ordinary holiness of the Godgift of sex and sexuality to the human family.

Our human sexuality is good . . .

God makes no mistakes. Everything God does comes from the greatest wisdom imaginable. We may look around our neighborhood or city or rural town and notice all kinds of flaws: Buildings may not match, roads may be too narrow, and dimly lit street corners that we once thought quaint may now be dangerous because of the darkness. When we design something, we often have to improve it later. But this is never the case with God. What God creates is good, is very good.

Human life is God's greatest creation on this earth. And the way we are created as human beings is also just right. God created us woman and man and this creation was very good. In a similar way, we can also affirm that the way new human life is created is also very good. God's designs are exquisite.

To put all this in simple terms, our identity as woman or man, as sexual persons, is very good—and very important. Human life is precious and holy. The community that preserves the value of human life is precious and holy. So also is that part of ourselves that creates and nurtures human life, our sexuality.

Human sexuality is an aspect of our personhood, an aspect that is present in every cell of our body. Human sexuality is everywhere within us. Our sexuality influences how we think, how we feel, how we respond to others, how we act. Whether married or single, we remain sexual persons.

We also know that our sexuality is a very vulnerable part of our life. It can be hurt or wounded or violated. In creating us sexual, God intended that our sexuality be that special part of ourselves that orients us to another, to someone different from ourselves. God created us woman or man, woman and man, woman with man, man with woman.

Rooted in our very being is a clue to our earthly life and to our final end. God created us not only for ourselves but also for others. God placed sexual attraction within us so that we will reach out across the boundaries of self to connect with others. In adolescence we begin to feel the power of this attraction. It both scares and excites us. Deep down we wonder what is going on within us. With faith, we know that what we are feeling are the wonderful and blessed workings of God.

Throughout life we remain under the influence of our sexuality. In our later years, we remain totally a woman or totally a man. Sexuality remains an important part of who each of us is until we breathe our last.

Sexuality, sex, and procreation

A holy, sacred action can embody God's deep love.

The sexual dimension of our humanity deeply influences us. This influence is lifelong and it affects us whether or not we are married. Yet we need to understand that in marriage God invites us to express our sexuality, particularly through actions that express marital love and through actions that can bring forth new human life. Through the act of sexual intercourse, married couples engage in a holy, a sacred, action that can embody both God's deep and faithful love as well as God's act of creating new life. The dignity of this human action is virtually incomparable to any other human act.

While the term *sexuality* refers to our identity as being either a woman or a man, the word *sex* can refer to those actions more specifically connected with the use of our sexual or reproductive organs. The Catholic Church teaches that these actions are reserved for marriage. The meaning or purpose of these actions is twofold: to express marital love and to be open to the creation of new life.

A careful reading of the writings of Vatican II provides a surprising answer to the question "How do new babies come to be?" Earlier church teaching, going back the last two centuries, said that new human life was the result of the sexual intercourse between the wife and the husband. New life was the biological result of a biological action.

While this is true, Vatican II felt this response to the question was too narrow. So the bishops have stated that the origin of human life is the love between the wife and the husband. Thus, human origins begin with more than biology. New life is the love of the couple. Or to go one step further, new life is their love expressing God's love.

The bishops have stated that the origin of human life is the love between the wife and the husband. Thus, human origins begin with more than biology. New life is the love of the couple. New life is their love expressing God's love.

Sexual love in marriage is a special kind of language—one of commitment and unconditional love. This love establishes an environment for the nurturing of new life. Thus, the church believes that married couples both procreate and nurture new life. The love of the family accompanies the growing child throughout life.

According to the church, the ideal home for a child is a loving two-parent household. Why? Because the complexity of a child, especially in its earlier years, requires caring attention and devotion and this can be more easily done by two than by one parent. The devotion and example of committed love brings children to understand the blessing of someday falling in love and entering a committed marital relationship.

However, a home without two parents can also raise children to be fully Christian. In fact, in any home in which children experience love, they experience the presence of a God who loves them no matter what.

A child living with only one parent can grow up with healthy, wholesome attitudes toward love and marriage. We make this happen if we are a single parent by exposing our child to other families in which parenting is shared. And this is a good thing for the Body of Christ because we all belong to each other.

Sexuality and responsibility

Sexual responsibility is connected with the creation and with the development of human life. We are to use our God-given sexuality in ways that respect God's intent. Part of that intent is that human sexuality be oriented to loving another. Sexuality is also a way we express a special kind of love, the love that is at the heart of marriage. To separate sexuality from that meaning is to step outside God's intent.

God's intent is that human sexuality be oriented to loving another—a way we express a special kind of love, the love that is at the heart of marriage.

In the official teachings of the church, the word *chastity* is used to describe the responsible use of our sexual expression. Chastity invites a proper integration of sexuality with all the other parts of our life.

Chastity, which invites us to be directed and disciplined, is a virtue both for the married and the unmarried. It combines respect and love for persons;

it serves life and all the processes relating to the creating and nurturing of life. Chastity affirms that God has created each human being as a sexual person. This virtue also helps us determine how to live as a sexual person in accord with God's intent for our happiness and perfection. In other words, how to understand our own sexuality—woman and man.

In order that Christian parents may worthily carry out their ministry, the synod fathers expressed the hope that a suitable catechism for families would be prepared.

Being sexually responsible also means we care for and educate our children. The church now considers this a special ministry. Because our families are the church of the home, those of us who are parents communicate the good news of salvation to children. The words of Pope John Paul II capture this dimension of family life quite well when he says:

> By virtue of their ministry of educating, parents are through the witness of their lives the first heralds of the gospel for their children. Furthermore, by praying with their children, by reading the word of God with them and by introducing them deeply through Christian initiation into the body of Christ—both the Eucharist and the ecclesial body—they become fully parents, in that they are begetters not only of bodily life but also of the life that through the Spirit's renewal flows from the cross and resurrection of Christ. In order that Christian parents may worthily carry out their ministry of education, the synod fathers expressed the hope that a suitable catechism for families would be prepared, one that would be clear, brief and easily assimilated by all.
>
> *(On the Family, 39)*

We parents have a special role in communicating our faith to our children. This is part of our ministry. This familystyle catechism is a direct response to the above invitation of the pope. It assists a family in its wonderful ministry where, in a sense, all Christian ministry begins.

"Everyone, man and woman, should acknowledge and accept his sexual identity. *Physical, moral, and spiritual* difference *and* complementarity *are oriented toward the goods of marriage and the flourishing of family life. The harmony of the couple and of society depends in part on the way in which the complementarity, needs, and mutual support between the sexes are lived out."* CCC, 2333

Our acceptance of our sexuality brings forth happiness in our children.

We have titled this chapter "The Wondrous Gift of Life, Love, and Sexuality" for one reason: The three are intricately connected. We are born into life to love and be loved, and this is a celebration of the wholeness of who we are—sexual beings.

Some people use the words *sex* and *sexuality* interchangeably. The two are closely related but, as we have already mentioned, they are not the same. We often refer to sex as the gender (man or woman) of a person. Or, we use the word to mean the actions of bodily sexual intimacy and pleasure we as males and females enjoy with one another. Sexuality, however, is the whole expression of our being either male or female. We are sexual beings even if we never have sex!

Some typical characteristics we attribute to the woman's sexual being are a gentleness of voice, a softness of body, a sensitivity to others, a deep intuition, an ability to recognize and respond to the feelings of others, a seemingly innate ability to nurture, and a spirituality. We label these characteristics as feminine; in reality, they are part of our wholeness, our sexuality—man and woman.

So, too, with the characteristics we attribute to the man's sexual being: strength of body; facial and chest hair; a deep, loud voice; a strong drive to protect and provide; and a spirituality. We label *these* characteristics as masculine. But they, too, are part of our wholeness, our sexuality—man and woman.

We often leave out the spiritual aspect of sexuality when we talk about males and females. Thus, we leave out how our sexuality—our wholeness—connects us to God. For through the wonderfulness of our differences, we find our oneness. Yes, each of us, male or female, have been given certain identifiable characteristics that seem to separate us, yet even within each of us, we find the "other" side of God.

Within each of us is a degree of the other, some characteristics we call feminine or masculine. And interestingly enough, that is one of the things that actually attracts us one to the other. For example, in a recent survey, women listed sensitivity as an important thing that attracts them to a man! (And usually we see sensitivity as a feminine trait.)

In this same survey, men listed a woman's ability to think for herself as a quality that strongly attracts them. (A male trait!) Interesting, isn't it? Blessed will be the time when we welcome our fullness as human beings—male and female—and when we allow this fullness to shine forth no matter what gender we happen to have been born. Then, and only then, will the image of God be truly visible to us. And we will no longer need to be worried about the battle of the sexes. We will have both won.

In the Old Testament, the book called "The Song of Songs" contains a collection of lyrical love songs. In them we find wonderful descriptions of sexuality and human beauty. These wedding songs are direct and they say what they say. And we frequently cannot tell, without help from biblical scholars, who—the male or the female—is saying what in these songs. Here is an example of how both share the same words:

> I hear my lover's voice. He comes running over the mountains, racing across the hills to me. . . . My lover speaks to me. Come then, my love; my darling, come with me. . . . You are like a dove that hides in the crevice of a rock. Let me see your lovely face and hear your enchanting voice.
>
> *(from Song of Songs 2:8, 10, 14)*

Actually, Scripture scholars attribute the first three sentences to the female and the last three, beginning with "Come then, my love," to the male. But either could say all of this. For our sexuality is composed of both male and female traits.

As members of families we are doing family ministry every day. And the primary lessons we teach our little boys and our little girls is how to be boy or girl. We carefully make sure our family ministry includes helping each child understand the image of God in the other: We all know that one of the biggest problems in marriage is not understanding and appreciating our differences. We can change that. We can understand and appreciate those God-given gifts!

If you have a two-parent household, do your children witness the gentle male and female love you demonstrate between you? Do they know that hugging and kissing and saying "I love you" is very much all right? Are you raising your children to be good lovers by showing them how to love one another with gentleness and generosity and kindness and thoughtfulness and life-giving humor?

Children live what they learn while growing up with you. As they live with you, are they living in a house of healthy affection between mom and dad?

If you live in a one-parent household, are you providing your little ones with healthy exposure to the image of God in the other gender? Do you talk about what being a loving man or woman means? Do you involve your children with happily married couples so that your children can see the strength and love between the two? Do you seek and find good materials to teach your children about love between men and women so their knowledge includes the grace of this reality? They can find in you the wonderful guidance of one part of the image of God, but they also need to know about the other.

A Psalm

May our sons in their youth be like plants that grow up strong. / May our daughters be like stately columns which adorn the corners of a palace. / May our barns be filled with crops of every kind. / May the sheep in our fields bear young by the tens of thousands. / May our cattle reproduce plentifully without miscarriage or loss. / May there be no cries of distress in our streets. / Happy is the nation of whom this is true; / happy are the people whose God is the LORD! *Psalm 144:12–15*

An Old Family Blessing

May your kids be healthy and good in school.
May they get fingerprints on your walls
And jelly on the floor.

May your house ring with the sounds of stereos,
Blow dryers, lawn mowers, dogs, and best friends.

May your floors be strewn with clothing, crayons.
May your phone ring with the voices of loved ones and strangers.

And may your home be blessed with readiness to sit right down and talk
Or play or cry or laugh with one another.

May your hearts be filled with understanding and forgiveness and a lot of time to just be.
May your little boys grow up to be loving men
Who share what's in their hearts as well as what's in their minds.
May your little girls grow up to be loving women
Who share their minds as well as their hearts.

May you celebrate the wonderfulness
Of being on God's earth at the same time,
In the same home,
In the unique experience of being your holy family.

Amen.

CHAPTER EIGHT
Fashioning a Better World—Creation Continues Through Us

A young girl responds to the needs of her universe . . .

Young people gathered in groups on the sidewalk. As the car pulled over and she hopped out, she felt so proud to be with them. The decision to come had been hard, but she knew the rally would be worth any effort she made.

Her parents worked hard for this town. She remembered how they were always doing something to make things better, and now her turn to help had come!

At first when she read about the rally, she thought it was just another "radical cause"—something to keep people busy! But then she walked along the creek herself, saw the debris, smelled the chemicals, and noted the absence of plants. In fact, she didn't see one living thing! That made her mad! People were right! Something had to be done.

So here she was, with hundreds of others, about to let that company know they had to stop—and not only that, they had to clean up the mess!

"We can't stand by any longer and let them poison our environment!" the organizers had said. "They're poisoning all of us!"

She knew it was true. It'd always been true. And enough was enough. Somehow, from the time she'd left college until now she'd grown in her awareness.

"This is it! God isn't going to create a new planet for us! It's up to us now! Our planet; our lives!" the placards proclaimed. The last part got to her. Because everything was connected; everyone was connected!

The best analogy she could draw was her family. All of them, from mom and dad down, even to their two sides of the family, and each member of these families was connected! It was the same with all of creation. Something like a family—all of it connected. And the time had come to make sure their families of the future had the beauty of the rest of creation to enjoy, as well as the beauty of the family!

"Respect for human dignity requires . . . the practice of solidarity, *in accordance with the golden rule and in keeping with the generosity of the Lord, . . ."*

CCC, 2407

Jesus preached his message to the people, using many other parables like these; he told them as much as they could understand. He would not speak to them without using parables, but when he was alone with his disciples, he would explain everything to them.

On the evening of that same day Jesus said to his disciples, "Let us go across to the other side of the lake." So they left the crowd; the disciples got into the boat in which Jesus was already sitting, and they took him with them. Other boats were there too. Suddenly a strong wind blew up, and the waves began to spill over into the boat, so that it was about to fill with water. Jesus was in the back of the boat, sleeping with his head on a pillow. The disciples woke him up and said, "Teacher, don't you care that we are about to die?"

Jesus stood up and commanded the wind, "Be quiet!" and he said to the waves, "Be still!" The wind died down, and there was a great calm.

Mark 4:33–39

Jesus responds to the cry of his disciples . . .

Can you imagine the shock when the wind and the waves obeyed Jesus? Some of the others on the boat must have wanted to jump ship after that occurrence!

Jesus always responded to his followers. Because they had grown used to this, they looked to Jesus, their leader and friend, to save their lives! They knew he could do something (anything!), so they awakened him. Then, after he had calmed the weather, he probably settled back down, closed his eyes, fell asleep again, and began to dream.

Many of us know how some weather threatens our lives: floods and tornadoes, hurricanes and avalanches.

Because of our abuse of the environment, the atmosphere of our planet is even beginning to threaten us. Jesus' disciples didn't worry about this, but we must.

How did Jesus face the threat to his friends? The best way he knew how; he calmed the wind and the waves. The teenager in our opening story is doing the same. She calms the seas that batter her environment; she stills the wind that refuses to listen to the pleas of the people. She acts against a threat to her brothers and sisters. She takes responsibility to make the world a better place.

The young woman acknowledges that something is polluting her world and that this will affect the generations of people who will come after her. So she does a very Christian thing: She joins in cleaning up the environment. Why is she protesting? Because she believes that the natural environment is worth saving. It sustains us; it speaks to us of God's love. Moreover, the young woman knows, as do we all, that we have only this universe. And like Jesus, we better be awake for this one!

> *"The seventh commandment enjoins respect for the integrity of creation. . . . Use . . . cannot be divorced from respect for moral imperatives."*
>
> CCC, 2415

Justice demands that we respond to the needs of our world.

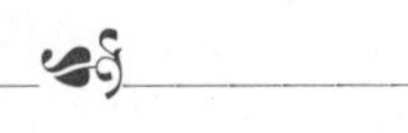

On any given day, we can hear many views about the future of the family: “The family today is in desperate straits. Its very survival is in question.” “The family is being torn apart by the pressures and demands of contemporary life.” “The family will soon be a museum, a social fossil from another era.” “We have to fix the family.”

These views are great attention-getters; all of us sit up and listen when someone announces with certainty and conviction that the end is near. We respond emotionally. “How terrible,” we think, “if the family should be lost!” In our hearts we recognize the singular importance of the family. It’s the glue that holds society together; family is the place where we can go to find security and safety from the dangers of the world. Most of us would agree that the loss of the family would be the greatest tragedy of modern times.

Usually the bearer of this horrible news follows the declaration with an analysis of what went wrong and who’s to blame for this unfortunate state of affairs. Well, who is to blame? Among the nominees are secularism, individualism, hedonism, consumerism, materialism, liberal capitalism, creeping socialism, the women’s movement, the men’s movement, the gay rights movement, two-paycheck families, television, rock music, sex, drugs, fast food restaurants, and the closing of the corner grocery store. We have lots to choose from!

But before we begin a lengthy discussion of who’s to blame for the demise of the family, let’s ask another question: If the family really dying? Or, are we simply seeing a “course adjustment” for the family as it makes its way as part of a rapidly changing society?

The jury on this may still be out, deliberating, debating. In some ways families *are* changing a great deal. They are smaller, more isolated from extended family. The divorce rate in our country is high; families are pulling into themselves, becoming more private; the number of single-parent families is increasing; and so on.

But in the midst of what seem to be negative trends, we can also identify some positive ones. What are they? The value of women and children has improved; marriage partners at odds with one another can now get professional help; the role of men as nurturers is expanding; educational levels are greater; members of families are healthier and, if illness comes, most can find help; we are less programmed to endure destructive social relations. We *can* change!

What all this means—both the negative and the positive trends—is that our family is not an island unaffected by the wider society. Of course the same can be said for each of us as individuals. We all live within a connected and complex social fabric; we cannot shut out the outside world. We need it and each other to survive as vital persons.

Given the influence of the social environment on our beliefs and values, we know that the "outside" plays a major role on what happens to our own person and to our family. So, both for self- and family-preservation, we must attend to what's happening "out there," because eventually we know it will "move inside."

In the words of Pope John Paul II, part of the family's role involves "participation in the development of society." When we do not participate in this development, social change influences us instead of our influencing it!

Family first and society next

The family is the basic unit of society and the interrelation between the family and society is mutual: they affect one another. The vitality of one is connected to the vitality of the other. In other words, the family changes society and society changes the family.

The family changes society and society changes the family.

This principle of mutual influence is at the heart of the social mission of the Christian family. Realizing how we affect society and how it affects our family, we begin to work for change. The young women in our opening story cares about the polluted creek. She realizes that she has a role to play in society and that she can make a difference. Accepting that challenge is the first step to making the world a better place for ourselves and for those who will come after us. And this is no small step to take.

According to the church, we are not just Christians. No. We are "Christians in the world." This means that our sanctity and our sanity come from our involvement in the many affairs of humankind. This is quite a turnabout for the church. In past times, it described the world as a waiting place, a fairly meaningless setting, where we lingered around before going to our real home—heaven. The church judged those who did "heavenly work" as more important than those who involved themselves only in "worldly tasks."

This attitude said that family life was insignificant when compared with "real" church activities. Of course, we now know that the family itself is church so this ill-founded division between church and family need no longer hinder us. Still, this appreciation and understanding of the domestic church—our family—is only beginning.

The word about the domestic church is out, but many have not understood and accepted it yet. Some few resist because they would just as soon keep their Christianity safely bounded by the property owned by their parish. But many, many others want to be in touch with the presence and activity of God in the life of the family. So they welcome the news that God is alive and well within our own family relationships.

In family, life begins; the family nourishes and nurtures life. But if we families are to survive and thrive, we must attend to the relationships within our family and we must involve ourselves in change in society.

Healthy families have "permeable boundaries." This image is one doctors use to describe a healthy cell. The wall of the cell can take in nourishment from outside the cell and eliminate waste products from the inside. Without this protective barrier, the cell would die. So, too, in the family.

The family can be a safe haven from the negative influences of the outside world. But if the family isolates itself in a total way, then it will lose the nourishment and vitality available from the outside. One example may suffice here: Some families do not have a television in their homes because they consider it an evil influence. But television can also be a wonderful way to access the world of art and music, drama and debate. Television can help the family; however, it can also harm. We must protect our family, yet we must use the good resources of society to nourish our families. We must have "permeable boundaries."

Hospitality and the family

Hospitality is a sign of God's openness to us.

The New Testament occasionally offers little indicators or lists (we might even call them checklists) for determining whether an individual or a community is on the right track in living the Christian life. We can often find the care of widows and orphans on these lists. Why? Because in ancient times, widows and orphans were without family ties.

In the time of Jesus, when a woman left her family to marry and her husband died, her original family did not take the woman and her children back. She would have to fend for herself, as would her children. They became totally vulnerable; their need was obvious.

Therefore, the early church encouraged Christian families to take widows and orphans under their care, as well as strangers, travelers, and others without homes. This reaching out was one of the first gestures of ministry in the church. Hospitality, or an openness to guests, was an important sign of God's openness to us.

After all, Jesus came to serve others, to wait on those gathered at the table, and even wash the feet of guests. After Jesus died and his presence entered into the members of the community, families took up his role of caregiver to the needy. Today, the needs of our neighbor call on our Christian response—a response rooted in justice.

Justice is the virtue by which we give everyone his or her due. Presently the world could improve its social justice. Why? Because the natural resources of the earth are poorly distributed; only a few possess the wealth of the world; rich nations still subjugate poor ones. Moreover, the citizens of some countries waste food by the ton while human beings in other countries die or survive only with scraps. Vast amounts of some nation's resources go into armaments to protect the investments and wealth of a few.

In recent years the church has heard the cry of the poor and has declared "a preferential option" for them. Because the poor, with their limited voice and power, seldom have the power to build up their own resources, we Christians must seek them out and serve them with generous hearts.

We must avoid doing this in a paternalistic way; that is, we must not pat the poor on the head and treat them like "good little children." Instead, we must help the poor and needy to help themselves. A simple statement illustrates why this is important: "Give a poor person a fish and that person will be hungry the next day; teach that person to fish and he or she will have food each day!"

In the United States, the bishops have initiated a program called the Campaign for Human Development. This program offers small grants to businesses and groups to help them get started on the road away from poverty and hopelessness. This program remains a wonderful sign of the generosity of Catholics in the United States, a sign of our concern for economic and social development among the less fortunate.

The bishops of the United States have written wonderful documents on the issue of peace and war and on the economic system in our own country and throughout the world. Slowly, the impact of these teachings is being felt within the church. Certainly, these documents, these issues, have a place in our family church too.

We need to keep in the forefront of our hearts two aspects of being Christian: (1) We are members of a community called the church; we share love among ourselves; we grow more like Jesus as our community works and prays and plays together. (2) As followers of Jesus, we must serve others; we must bring the love of God to others; we must know no bounds in our service and assistance to the needy. By that, we mean those who need material and spiritual help.

We Christians reach the fullness of life when we incorporate in our lives a healthy blend of love of God, love of neighbor, and love of self. And we need to do this both in the church of our home, as well as in the broader church.

The response of one can change our world for the better.

Sensitivity to the effects of our living on the earth is a relatively new awareness for humanity. Every other living thing on earth just goes about its natural God-given way of being a creature or a plant or other life force, like the sun or the moon. Except for us. We—part of the creation gifted with the most intelligence—have brought damage to the rest of creation.

We have upset the balance, the plan. We have hurt our home—the earth—and we are beginning to mess up outer space. And most certainly, we have also hurt the other residents of earth—the rest of God's living creations.

Before the last few decades, we weren't aware that our actions could spoil our environment, that we were "fouling our own nest." Just as we didn't know that cigarettes caused cancer or that blood could transmit the HIV virus. We didn't have that knowledge then; we do now. And we have made great strides since becoming aware.

Every day new knowledge comes to us about how we affect one another and our environment. More and more we are aware of our interconnectedness; nothing separates us. We are one.

Many of us have started to do whatever we can to help bring change to our world. We are trying to reverse the damage to our delicate home, the earth. Most of us do some form of recycling of household materials because our communities began some sort of program. Some of us even did so before a community said we had to recycle. Some families educate themselves about their own neighborhoods and communities. They initiate changes to care more for the earth around them.

We live at a time when humanity has learned that its actions affect the universe, and we are trying to reverse the damage we have caused. We are blessed to live at a time when we can do something about the tragedies we have created. We can do something not just for ourselves, but for our future family members—all those great, great grandkids or cousins and their families whom we will never know and all the other little faces we see on TV or in the supermarket with eyes that reflect their vulnerability.

Families caring for other families and for the home in which we all live is a wonderful Christian response to our God's love for us. In hundreds of little (and big) ways we can make a difference. Making the world a better place to live starts with little decisions to make the small world around us a better place to live.

Remember the wonderful little story of the little boy at the seashore? Each day he would walk from his home to the beach where he would perform life-saving activities. You see, there were many starfish in the waters near his home. The waves would wash them onto the beach and if a starfish was "beached," it would surely die because the hot sun would dry it out. The little boy's project was simple. Whenever he spotted a washed-in starfish, helpless on the drying sand, he would gently toss it back to its life-supporting habitat in the sea. An older beachcomber happened by one day and watched the little boy scurrying about, "saving lives," as the boy would say. How futile, how wasteful of time and energy, thought the man. And so, out of his sense of duty to correct the little boy, he simply informed him about the thousands, maybe millions, of stranded starfish on the beaches of the world.

"It will make no difference," he said, "if you spend all your days and nights saving only a small number of the starfish."

The little boy tried to fathom the wisdom of the man but to no avail. So once again, he reached down and hurled a recently arrived starfish back into the sea and said to the man, "To this one, it does make a lot of difference!"

Still, some of us don't do anything for our home, the earth, yet. We think our actions—the actions of one person, one family—make little difference. But let's remember the words of an old song: "It is better to light just one little candle, than to curse the darkness." We can light those flickering candles; we can bring light to our family and to our home and to our planet. This is a simple matter of addition. One of us and one of us and one of us make three of us. And a million of these ones can together make a strong force for good.

Perhaps our precious household, even if we live alone, can find one more way to help.

"'The Church's love for the poor . . . is a part of her constant tradition.' This love is inspired by the Gospel of the Beatitudes, of the poverty of Jesus, and of his concern for the poor. Love for the poor is even one of the motives for the duty of working so as to 'be able to give to those in need.' It extends not only to material poverty but also to the many forms of cultural and religious poverty."

CCC, 2444

A Psalm

Lord God Almighty, none is as mighty as you; / in all things you are faithful, O Lord. / You rule over the powerful sea; you calm its angry waves. / You crushed the monster Rahab and killed it; / with your mighty strength you defeated your enemies. / Heaven is yours, the earth also; you made the world and everything in it. / You created the north and the south; / Mount Tabor and Mount Hermon sing to you for joy. . . .

How happy are the people who worship you with songs, / who live in the light of your kindness!

Psalm 89:8–12, 15

Kinda Hard to Understand

You'll excuse us, Lord Jesus,
But there's one big question,
And we feel so comfortable with you
That we know you won't mind our asking.

How come if you could calm the seas
And turn five loaves into five thousand
And water into premium wine
How come, well—how come you seem to have quit?

The earth is in trouble! You must know that, Lord.
And sometimes it seems you don't care.
Well, sometimes it seems like that, Lord!

Now, we know you're around here.
We feel you all the time.
We can't look at a flower or touch a newborn's cheek
Without thinking of you.
But it's confusing, Lord, because newborns are dying
Or not even being allowed to be born!
The earth is in big trouble!

Now, Lord Jesus, it isn't that we doubt you're here,
So, um . . . m . . . we wondered . . .
Could you maybe get a little more involved
Like you were for those other folks?

OH? You are? Through us?
Well, okay then. Our turn. Amen.

CHAPTER NINE

Loving God Above All Else

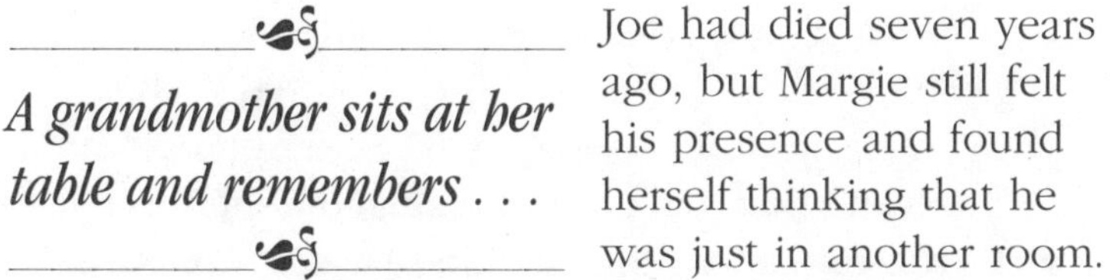

A grandmother sits at her table and remembers . . .

Joe had died seven years ago, but Margie still felt his presence and found herself thinking that he was just in another room.

She knew he wasn't in the bedroom or in the bathroom or even outside in the yard. But she still expected him. She'd heard that when you lost someone close—and she and Joe had been married almost fifty years—you had this feeling. You felt your loved one was still near, in the house, in the next room.

But Margie was the one who was really still here. Sometimes she wondered why Joe went first. In fact, sometimes she even wondered why he *got* to go first! Being left here without him wasn't easy. The house was so quiet most of the time. (Especially since he was the one who made a lot of the noise!) And sometimes she felt so alone.

And so today she sat, somewhat lonely, at the family table—the place where she read and did bills and was ready for anyone who came to visit. Ready to listen. She knew that one of her greatest gifts was her ability to listen. She just tried to really hear what family and friends were saying to her, to catch hold of the feelings they didn't always express. She tried to be here for them—ready to sympathize and encourage, to laugh and cry. Oh, she could write volumes about the stories she'd heard at this table!

She began to remember some of her own stories, stories that happened when she was young and beautiful. She remembered falling in love with the best looking Irishman in the high school; she remembered having such great times with him and their friends in the little hometown. She thought of all the good times before and after they married, especially the kids.

She remembered hard times, too—the three miscarriages, too many kids sometimes, too little money. Funny, she even remembered those early days when she'd worn an apron every day with a housedress and a girdle, no less! "Boy, have times changed," she thought. "I can't even remember the last time I wore a dress! Probably for Erin's wedding," she thought as she remembered her granddaughter.

Suddenly she was remembering other celebrations: Marty's wedding and the party at Joey's house; Johnny's wedding and the champagne cork that hit his eye; her daughter's reception at Gracie's; Danny's wedding and the reception at the hotel. Joey's wedding and the trick his brother Larry played on him. Then she thought of Larry and his "celebration"—his kidney transplant. How glad he was to be off that dialysis machine!

Her thoughts moved forward and backward. She remembered the times—so many of them—when the whole family got together. Time after time, a host of family filled her kitchen. "The amount of food Joe and I put out would feed an army!" she thought.

Then, she mused for a few moments. "I wouldn't trade a minute of my life for anything!" she thought. "Not a minute. The two of us did so good! *I* did so good! I have such great kids! If I died tomorrow it'd be okay. But even if I live, it's still okay. God knows I might still have work to do!"

"Hi, Mom," her youngest son said as he came in with his youngest son, "Whatcha' doin'?"

"Hi, Gramma!" Matt said. "Can I have some juice?"

"Sure, if daddy says so," she wisely answered, smiling at the little face that looked like Grandpa Joe.

"Then the King will say to the people on his right, 'Come, you that are blessed by my Father! Come and possess the kingdom which has been prepared for you ever since the creation of the world. I was hungry and you fed me, thirsty and you gave me a drink; I was a stranger and you received me in your homes, naked and you clothed me; I was sick and you took care of me, in prison and you visited me.' The righteous will then answer him, 'When, Lord, did we ever see you hungry and feed you, or thirsty and give you a drink? When did we ever see you a stranger and welcome you in our homes, or naked and clothe you? When did we ever see you sick or in prison, and visit you?' The King will reply, 'I tell you, whenever you did this for one of the least important of these followers of mine, you did it for me!' "

Matthew 25:34–40

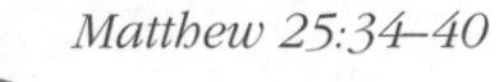

Jesus tells us that God remembers all the love we share with others, in Jesus' name . . .

In this scriptural passage, Jesus gives us a clear job description—a simple way to live. Jesus tells us how God wants us to respond to our world and the people in it. And the "how" seems so simple. In fact, if this passage were a job description, evaluating our "performance" against these criteria would be a piece of cake!

The poetic passage describes the reality of caring for one another. It mentions all the ordinary needs of life—food, water, clothing, shelter, care when sick, and someone to take away the loneliness. The very basics of human needs.

The passage invites and challenges us to see God in everyone (everyone!), even "the least important." (And only God can judge that, and God sees us as equal.)

Seeing the beauty of God in a helpless newborn is easy. In fact, seeing the beauty of God in a new husband or wife doesn't take much effort either!

And doing something for those in whom we see God isn't always hard either. We easily put a dollar or two in the collection basket or a bit of loose change in the Salvation Army's red pail at the grocery store. Donating our leftovers, our discards to charitable organizations that help the "least important" doesn't take much effort from us—just cleaning out and cleaning up the house! That's all!

But Jesus didn't come to say that responding to God's presence in others would be easy. No. He said that it would be hard often, sometimes very hard. Moreover, we would probably rather do anything else than that which he invites us to do. But those of us who hear his word about God's kingdom want to do this. Why? Because Jesus has said that this is how God's children love. And this *is* how we love. Especially in family.

For most of us, loving within our family represents much of our response to this passage from Scripture. The woman in our opening story—an elderly grandmother, even a great grandmother, a widow, a mother, a sister, a friend—was once a young woman, a new bride. And she held those newborns, one after another after another, and cared for them when they needed her. And other times she even laid in bed bleeding from other children who didn't get to share their life with Margie and Joe and the rest of the family.

This grandmother once had a handsome new bridegroom and the world was their oyster! And now he is gone, and she is left behind. And life is hard at times, but also wonderfully fulfilling. She finds herself greatly loved, but nonetheless alone. And her memories come—of giving food and water, clothing and shelter; of welcoming many and all strangers; of caring for sickness and visiting those unable to come to her. And when she and God are ready, her place with God is ready for her.

Blessed are those whose lives are filled with memories of loving others.

God remembers love . . .

What was there in the beginning? Space? Chaos? Nothing?

No. In the beginning, was love. Before anything or anyone crossed from nothing to something, love shimmered, glimmered, beckoned, welcomed. Love is the family from which all of us came, and the family to which all of us will go. And that is the power, the field of energy, that surrounds every family today. We may not always see the energy of this love, but we always pray it is there. Among the saddest of all realities is when, in a family, love is lacking.

In our opening story, we read about a woman reminiscing. We sat with her and enjoyed her happy memories of family life and love. We know that she has made a difference in her world. And we give thanks. We've seen the faces of other older people. Their faces are lost in thought with a hint of a smile around the mouth and a gleam in the eyes. They are here with us, but they are also back in their memories, somewhere in the past, bathed in thoughts of thousands of meals with family, of meals with candles or babies on the table, of meals with plain old tomato soup and cheese sandwiches or beef stroganoff (which some of the kids won't even try!).

These memories celebrate life. These times may have come only once, but our heart, living them, captures them forever like a camera and we are able to pull them out of the photo album of our heart's love and celebrate our family. And even if we don't remember them all, God does. God remembers how we lived our love, shared it with others, and grew holy and wholesome; God remembers how we followed the example of Jesus.

What is our reward for doing this? Jesus knew that this life, while often deeply happy, is still incomplete.

Jesus, who hungered himself, knew that hunger for more remains within each of us. As Christians, we are blessed in knowing (at least in a small way) the origin of that hunger. We crave the Absolute; we long for Good; we seek Love. Our hunger is the gravitational pull back to where we came from. It is God's call to return to our first home in God's heart.

Metaphorical language? Poetics? Yes, it has to be. For neither eye nor ear has witnessed what God has prepared for us who know how to love. So we cannot draw the whole picture. We can only embrace it from the standpoint of hope, yet we hold this dream as very real.

And as our days grow less and less, we sometimes pause and wonder. Like old people at kitchen tables and young people coming in a door. Near the beginning and toward the end of our lives, our awareness of the mystery in which we live seems to have more impact. But the mystery of God's love and our longing for more is always with us. So taking time to pause (like now) and reflect on God's great love for each of us may be a wonderful thing to do.

God's work and God's play

On the seventh day, God looked over all . . . and gently sank into the biggest, most comfortable rocking chair ever made.

In the Catholic tradition, we find two parallel ways to spend time: We can work or we can play. And both forms of activity are serious. We work in imitation of God who created the universe and enlisted our help to perfect it. So we build homes and grow food and work at computers. Most of the time most people work.

But on the seventh day, God looked over all that was made in the workshop, smiled, put down the tools and gently sank into the biggest, most comfortable rocking chair ever made. (This detail is not mentioned in the Bible!) God was overheard saying that *doing* is fine, but *being* is even better. When God gave the Ten Commandments to Moses, number three was "Keep Holy the Sabbath." After the resurrection of Jesus, Christians moved number three to what we call the eighth day of creation because this was the day that God raised Jesus from death. This event began a new era, thus a new day.

For Christians the holy Sabbath (Saturday) moved to Sunday, which became the day of the Lord. Soon the young church of the apostles and martyrs met on Sundays to celebrate the breaking of the bread, which they called their agape—their meal of love. We know this as the Mass, or the Eucharist. Like the Sabbath for the Jews, Sunday became a special day for Christians.

Once Christianity came out of the catacombs (where the followers of Jesus had gone to worship during the Roman persecutions), the early Christians established a new practice on Sunday: They prohibited servile work. Christians believed strongly in the freedom Jesus had won for them through his death and resurrection. To symbolize their new condition, they didn't work on Sunday. Instead, they played just as God had! They believed that their play was a special gift from God who had given them a day to celebrate life in its fullest. They set aside the mundane concerns of the day-to-day world. *Being* replaced *doing*!

Have we kept this wonderful tradition of our church? Do we gather with other believers to remember Jesus in the breaking of the bread? Is Sunday any different from the rest of the week for us? Do we allow ourselves the time to pray *and* to play? God asks us to do so. Yet we seldom discuss this. When was the last time we heard a sermon on the need to play? When did we hear that not to play is against the law and against the wishes of God? When did we hear that God wants us to rejoice in life, to shout "Amen! Alleluia! Yippie!"

God knows us very well. And one of the things God knows is that we need a balance in our life between work and play. God set up the week to allow for this to happen.

Banquets and family meals

Jesus says to us, "When you break bread together, remember me." We do this at our family meals—around the table or at the counter. Anytime a celebration of love happens, we are remembering Jesus; we are making him present.

The Old Testament often describes the time of the longed-for Messiah in terms of a banquet at which the guests have plenty of food to eat, wine to drink, and good conversation to enjoy. In the Gospel according to John, Jesus' first miracle was his changing water into wine at Cana in Galilee. The early readers of John's Gospel, those who knew the Old Testament too, would know immediately that more was going on at that wedding feast than meets the eye. The time of our salvation was dawning; the Messiah was near. And because of this good news, a time had come for feasting, not fasting. This miracle announced that the good times had come! The best of times!

About three years after this feast in Cana, John's Gospel takes us to another banquet, one in Jerusalem. An upper room there had been prepared for the Passover feast. During the entire year, no meal was more important for Jewish people, and Jesus and his friends were Jews. They looked forward to good food, good drink, and good conversation.

And at this banquet, Jesus changed bread and wine into his body and blood. Just as God had provided daily food for the ancient Israelites when they wandered in the desert, so Jesus gave his followers nourishment for the journey. But at this last supper, Jesus showed us that his food is not just for the day's consumption; it is forever. The banquet (which is the kingdom) has begun and it will not end. The celebration is eternal.

At this last supper, Jesus used the words, "Do this in memory of me." Memories are forever. God holds in gentle hands all the love that enlightens our memories. The opening story of this chapter gives us a hint of this. Lifetime memories are food for the soul of the grandmother in our story.

Jesus is also our memory. He says to us, "When you break bread together, remember me." We do this at our family meals—around the table or at the counter. And at times, like Margie in our story, we remember someone at the breaking of our bread. This can even happen at picnics or with pizza in front of the TV or at other special times when we share a meal. (Even, perhaps, as family at a good old fast food restaurant!) Anytime a celebration of love happens, we are remembering Jesus; we are making him present.

So a lot is going on at meals, especially family meals, if our minds are attuned to the great mysteries of life. And meals include goodies with Grandma in the afternoon while watching our favorite purple dinosaur. Jesus has assured us that when two or three are gathering in his name, he is in their midst. These are important words of Jesus. They alert us to a presence and a power that is not readily experienced. When we enter this experience, however, with faith (heart open, eyes wide, ears alert), more is apt to happen to us. Banquets can happen anywhere.

The final judgment

Hearing the gospel can be scary.

We read in the scriptural story for this chapter of the last judgment. This time of reckoning will reveal all that happened in our life—those events of which we were aware at the time; those events that slipped our notice; those events that cause us to smile in remembrance; those events that cause us to grimace.

This judgment account focuses sharply on the practical implications of the law of love. Attend to each other's needs, Jesus tells us, for within every hungry, thirsty, naked, lonely, or homeless person you will find God, waiting for your love. We must reach out and do for another simply because this person needs to feel the touch of God's love and God gives that love through us. How lucky we are! We can give God's love to one another!

Hearing this gospel can be scary for it seems to imply that those who did not respond to the human needs of neighbors are going to be "blindsided." If they had known that God was reaching out to them, calling out to them, in another, they would have been at the front of the line of volunteers. They would do anything for God! Anything! But for others? Well, that's a different story.

But the Gospel speaks truth. And the job description is very clear.

As we conclude this book on the Christian life, consider the challenges it sets before us. In every (every! every! every!) moment of our waking life, God invites us to express Christian love and concern. Our love begins with our family. If we do not respond to the needs of family members with the care that Jesus would give them, then we've missed the boat! But our love must extend beyond family to the far reaches of the world. We must extend our love to the edge of God's love, and God loves to the edge of the universe and beyond.

God remembers the love we gave to others around our family table of worship.

Kitchen tables are such holy places. Someone once wrote that more happens around a kitchen table than anywhere else where humans hang out. Not only do we prepare food here, we also feed the hungry and give drink to the thirsty. Moreover, the holy experience of sharing our stories happens at the tables where we share our lives. One person reports a bit of her or his experience from that day at school or at the job or in the store or the yard or wherever. Someone else comments, then another voice pipes up! Around the table, we tell one story after another about our separate journeys; we bring the world into our home and find its meaning for us there.

We bring in new family members so they learn how to do this thing called "family" around our table. As soon as we can prop up the baby in a highchair, we place the chair near the table so the baby can feel a sense of being part of this holy community. We want our children to understand that coming together this way is important; we want them to value coming to the table to eat and be together, because this is one of the ways we are church.

The table is often the gathering place for visitors to our home, which is the domestic church. At the table, we welcome strangers into our midst. And, of course, we offer them refreshments—coffee, tea, beer, popcorn, store-bought cookies. These offerings are a holy symbol of our caring. Then we "break bread" by discussing the latest cars or sports events or good sales or by expressing our concerns about the weather or the world or the three gray hairs we discovered this morning! What is happening here? God's love is being shared, passed one to the other, broken open in Jesus' name.

And there's more. Tables are more than places to eat or drink or visit. They make the best homework and sewing and build-it-before-tomorrow-school-project places. We construct tons of crafts on tables as we test and share our gifts of creativity. We lay newborns on tables to change their smelly diapers; we coo at them and delight them with rattles.

At our table, we do other holy family business like figuring our taxes; paying bills; writing letters; using the computer or typewriter; sorting and folding clothes; and even, from time to time, carefully covering the table's surface, placing a chair on top of it, and then painting a piece of furniture to give pleasure to another family member.

One of the most special ministries that happens at the table is the ministry of listening when a loved one is in pain. One of us listens to another share the sadness or loneliness or frustrations or anger or hurt or struggle of just trying to get through this life in one piece. Listening at the table with open arms and heart is a holy time, for in the midst of us is Jesus, showing us how to listen with love. And more often than not, the table is witness to times of holy healing as tears bless it's well-used surface and someone forgives another.

Of course, tables are only material, lifeless structures. What brings life to the table are the people who gather around it doing all those things we just mentioned. To sit at table with someone is to establish and affirm human connectedness. And this is the holiest thing of all.

Listening and talking, drinking and eating—simple, yet not so simple. Nourishing our bodies and nourishing our souls. And, most important of all, nourishing the bonds between us. We need to eat in order to survive. We need to eat together to live. Is it no wonder that when our Scriptures speak of our final place, it is at a banquet, a banquet more scrumptious than one ever experienced? and it will certainly be interesting to find out who's sitting next to us. It sure will!

Blessed indeed is the place we share our meals. And blessed are the holy memories soaked into the tabletop.

Perhaps some of us have never thought of our table as a holy place, as the altar of our home. Perhaps the next time we adorn it with a tablecloth, candles, flowers, and our best everyday dishes and surround it with those we love and who love us, we might consider blessing that holy place.

"Faith in God's love encompasses the call and the obligation to respond with sincere love to divine charity. The first commandment enjoins us to love God above everything and all creatures for him and because of him."

CCC, 2093

A Psalm

Praise the Lord! / Praise the Lord, my soul! / I will praise him as long as I live; / I will sing to my God all my life. / Happy are those who have the God of Jacob to help them. / and who depend on the Lord their God, / the Creator of heaven, earth, and sea, / and all that is in them. / He always keeps his promises; / he judges in favor of the oppressed / and gives food to the hungry. / The Lord sets prisoners free and gives sight to the blind. / He lifts those who have fallen; / he loves his righteous people. / He protects the strangers who live in our land; / he helps widows and orphans, / but takes the wicked to their ruin. / The Lord is king forever. / Your God O Zion, will reign for all time.

Psalm 146:1–2, 5–10

Family Sabbath Prayer

Yes, to the Day of the Lord
When we pause for prayer and praise
In church buildings and forest walks.

Yes, to the Day of Rest
In bed, on couches, in hammocks
On the beach, in the water, in parks.

Yes, to the Day of Games
On fields, in fairways, on courts,
In the stands for the fans.

Yes, to the Day of Friends—
Old ones and new ones,
Time wasted in talk and story telling.

Yes, to the Day of Family
Moms, dads, kids, cousins, grandfolk
Being family.

That's living
In the sunshine of our God.
A slice of heaven,
A moment of forever.
Amen.